Calvin

LANCASTER PAMPHLETS

Calvin

Michael Mullett

ROUTLEDGE
London and New York

First published 1989 by Routledge
11 New Fetter Lane, London EC4P 4EE
29 West 35th Street, New York, NY 10001

© *1989 Michael Mullett*

Photoset by Rowland Phototypesetting Ltd
Bury St Edmunds, Suffolk
and printed in Great Britain by
Richard Clay Ltd, Bungay, Suffolk

British Library Cataloguing in Publication Data
Mullett, Michael A.
Calvin.
1. *Reformed churches. Calvin, Jean, 1509–1564*
I. Title   II. Series
284'.2'0924

Library of Congress Cataloging-in-Publication Data
Mullett, Michael A.
Calvin / Michael Mullett.
p. cm. – (Lancaster pamphlets)
Bibliography: p.
1. *Calvin, Jean, 1509–1564.   2. Reformation–Biography.*
I. Title.   II. Series.
BX9418.M83   1989
284'.2'092—dc20   89-6299
[B]

ISBN 0-415-00057-2

IN MEMORIAM
Charles James Lancaster

Contents

Foreword

Lancaster Pamphlets offer concise and up-to-date accounts of major historical topics, primarily for the help of students preparing for Advanced Level examinations, though they should also be of value to those pursuing introductory courses in universities and other institutions of higher education. Without being all-embracing, their aims are to bring some of the central themes or problems confronting students and teachers into sharper focus than the textbook writer can hope to do; to provide the reader with some of the results of recent research which the textbook may not embody; and to stimulate thought about the whole interpretation of the topic under discussion.

At the end of this pamphlet is a list of works, most of them recent or fairly recent, which the writer considers most important for those who wish to study the subject further.

Introduction: the importance of Calvin and Calvinism

By the time of Martin Luther's death in 1546 some of the earlier vigour of the first, Lutheran, phase of the Protestant Reformation had begun to fade. Lutheranism had been expanding territorially, chiefly in Germany and Scandinavia, ever since the mid-1520s, but had been doing so largely under the protection of city and state governments. Thus the Lutheran movement, which had first erupted after 1517 as a nationwide explosion of protest in Germany, had turned into a set of regional established Churches and had lost much of its earlier exciting aura of social and religious renewal. Indeed, there was serious doubt, above all on the part of Luther himself, about the extent to which the Lutheran Reformation had reformed Germany at all, raised real levels of religious instruction or improved morals. At the same time, the Lutheran churches had become chronically and unattractively divided over theology.

These defects were all the more serious since from the mid-1540s onwards the Catholic Church, which had been gravely weakened by Luther's revolt, was beginning to put its house in order, with its great reforming Council of Trent opening in 1545.

In this decade of the 1540s, when a shadow fell across the future of Luther's Reformation, the most important member of the second generation of reformers following after Luther began to attract increasing international attention. This was the Frenchman John Calvin, the reformer of the city of Geneva. Calvin's contributions to

1

the Reformation were the following: he evolved a Protestantism that could operate independently of state support or defy hostile state authority; he equipped this form of Protestantism with a supple and resilient church organization of its own; he endowed it with a clear, un-mystical, intellectually coherent theology; and he injected into it a strong element of personal and social moral discipline. In all these ways, Calvin was able to compensate for certain shortcomings in the Lutheran prototype of the Protestant Reformation. Where Protestantism might have seemed about to go on the defensive against a renascent Catholic Church, Calvin made the Reformation once again an aggressive force for change.

1

Religion and the Church in early sixteenth-century France

John Calvin's early religious upbringing took place within the Catholic Church of early sixteenth-century France, a Church desperately in need of the reform that became the theme of Calvin's life. Looked at first of all from the institutional point of view, the Church in France reflected the key importance of the monarchy in national life. Indeed, in common with other western European states such as England, France was showing a marked tendency to wrest ecclesiastical control out of the hands of the papacy and to nationalize the Church as a royal institution in one kingdom. This process, in France as elsewhere, was particularly to the fore in the vital areas of finance and of senior ecclesiastical appointments, the latter being especially important since kings felt they needed reliable and serviceable men to staff a kingdom's bishoprics. Under the terms of the 1516 Concordat of Bologna, an agreement negotiated with the papacy, the French Crown nominated ten archbishops and eighty-two bishops in France's numerous episcopate.

The Crown did not, however, exercise complete freedom of choice over ecclesiastical appointments. France was an aristocratic society as well as a monarchical polity and the composition of the episcopate partly reflected the predominance of the nobility in French life. Certain noble families exercised effective monopolies over appointments to bishoprics and other lucrative ecclesiastical benefices within their areas of influence and they regularly inserted younger sons into those positions. Thus leaders of the French Church were recruited on the basis of a spoils system that took account primarily of financial priorities, of aristocratic privilege and of the political needs of the Crown, especially its need to reward loyal supporters and state servants with ecclesiastical revenues. Such a system, obviously, could not be guaranteed to produce dedicated pastoral clergy having spiritual vocations. That said, this rickety system did, perhaps surprisingly, produce some clerics of holy lives and high ideals. Such a one was Bishop Guillaume Briçonnet of Meaux (1470–1533). With regard to his background, Briçonnet's appointment was not a promising one in terms of the increasingly urgent tasks of Church reform. Son of a Crown servant and a former royal ambassador, Briçonnet was a pluralist – a collector of Church benefices – and a classic product of the spoils system. Yet Briçonnet set in motion an ambitious and partially successful plan of preaching and reform in his Meaux diocese. The Concordat system was not necessarily inimical to Church reform.

Yet there was pressing need for such reform. Much of the *malaise* stemmed from the ingrained habit of regarding an ecclesiastical appointment not as a vocation to service but more as a bundle of personal rights, privileges and receipts. From this arose resistance to all change, fierce defence of one's existing status and constant appeals to precedent against reform. In 1501, for instance, the Cardinal d'Amboise, backed by the Crown and the papacy, attempted to make the Cordelier monks of Paris observe their own rule. He was checked not only by the monks' no doubt infuriating habit of chanting psalms whenever he tried to talk to them, but also by their even more effective tactic of quoting their ancient charters as a bar to any reform whatsoever.

There seemed to be also a pervasive and debilitating disputatiousness about the French Church. Calvin's own father provides us with one very typical example, becoming involved in a protracted financial quarrel with the cathedral chapter of his home city of Noyon, a dispute which led to his excommunication. This rift may have had some influence on John Calvin's own alienation from the Catholic Church. The way in which institutional religion confirmed the habits of a quarrelsome society was deeply unsettling because of the function which Christian religion was supposed to exercise of instilling social peace.

Peacemaking was certainly regarded in French popular culture and in popular mentalities as an important social function of religion and its rituals. On the major feast of Christ in the Eucharist, *Corpus Christi*, to take one example, neighbours were expected to entertain and regale one another and in the process extinguish a year's disputes in this annual festival of communion. Indeed, ordinary French men and women seem to have regarded religion as at least in part a system for ordering and controlling their environment and regulating their communities. They needed patrons and protectors to see them through this life's vicissitudes and these they found in the myriad saints of the Church. Most of these were held to have specialist functions which qualified them as patrons of particular groups, especially occupational groups, or alternatively their specialisms were invoked in particular emergencies such as loss of money. All this was part of a magical or miraculous apparatus for controlling the material environment in this life as well as for ensuring salvation in the world to come: it meant using super-nature to influence nature. It could lead to some quite bizarre manifestations: in the Dombes region of south-east France, women with sick children would invoke the aid of a folk saint, Guinefort, whom they assimilated to a mythic figure of a child-protecting dog.

That was, though, only an exaggerated development of a tendency still strongly evident in popular piety throughout Europe on the eve of the Reformation, a tendency to use religion to get things done in the material world. This impulse had traditionally been sanctioned by the official Church, with its prayers, masses and rituals to protect crops, ensure good weather, cure sickness, and in general effect a permanent cycle of miracles. However, in the period we are considering we can detect a trend, not always consciously articulated or even consciously present, whereby educated elites were moving towards the greater spiritualisation and de-materialisation of religion, making it much more a matter of personal salvation in an after-life – the issue that haunted the theology of Luther and of Calvin. This salvation of souls was, of course, earned for man by Christ alone, and the saints, dear as they were to popular religion as agents of material assistance in this life, played no part in winning eternal life. They were to be relentlessly eliminated from Calvin's scheme of essentially spiritual salvation, but even before that enlightened reformists were pouring scorn on the superstitions associated with the saint-cult – 'superstition' here meaning belief in daily beneficial miracles performed by invoked saints. A less superstitious Christianity was beginning to make headway, partly associated with Calvin's mentor, Erasmus.

2

Christian humanism

John Calvin's education took place against the background of a long-term intellectual revolution. The prevailing academic system of theology in medieval Europe and its universities is known as scholasticism. Classic scholasticism twinned the methods of the ancient Greek philosopher Aristotle with the Christian Scriptures so as to produce a synthesis of revealed Christian faith and human reason. This scholasticism flourished in the hands of such masters as St. Thomas Aquinas (1225–74). In the fourteenth century the scholastic synthesis broke down. A new movement within scholasticism, known as Nominalism, undermined the reliance on reason that had been the hallmark of classic scholasticism. In place of reason, the Nominalists placed emphasis on ecclesiastical authority and on Scripture as the primary means of attaining the knowledge of God – a stress on Scripture which reached a high point in the movement known as Christian humanism. In the fifteenth and early sixteenth centuries, the alleged sterilities of scholasticism came to be widely discredited and indeed ridiculed, amongst humanist intellectuals.

Initially, humanism was a trend originating in later medieval Italy concerned with the rediscovery, editing, and publication of the main texts of ancient Greek and Latin literature. There was even a paganistic tinge to this literary humanism, which was, after all, a movement of deference to the norms of the ancient, pagan world. Even when they were not overtly neo-paganistic, humanist scholars could be harshly critical of accepted Catholic values and assumptions. Thus the archetypal fifteenth-century Italian humanist scholar, Lorenzo Valla, through his work in the field of literary editing of early documents, undermined the textual legitimation of the pope's temporal rule.

With all this criticism of corruption and of debased intellectual methods, many Italian humanist scholars of the Renaissance were aiming at a new synthesis, one between Christianity and pre-Christian philosophies such as that of Plato. Humanism – love of the classics – linked to Christianity produced the most exciting new intellectual development in Europe on the eve of the Reformation, Christian humanism. The acknowledged leader of this movement was the Dutchman Desiderius Erasmus (1466–1536), the scourge of scholastic traditionalists, of obscurantist monks and of all those who traded in the lucrative superstitions of popular piety. An outstanding Latin scholar, Erasmus made it his business to recover the earliest sources of Christianity – the early Church fathers of theology, and, beyond them, the Scripture, especially the New Testament, to whose study Erasmus was passionately dedicated. The outcome of his scriptural scholarship was his 1516 edition, along with a new Latin translation, of the New Testament in its original Greek. Although Erasmus remained essentially a Catholic – a critical one – the tendency of his New Testament edition was to undermine many features of current Catholicism. To cite just one example, Erasmus's disclosure of the Greek basic text of the New Testament revealed that the original meaning of a key New Testament concept, repentance, was not the formal Catholic practice of doing penance for sins but rather an interior change of heart.

As part of the Christian humanist recourse to Scripture of which Erasmus was the leading light there was a re-awakening of interest in the seminal Christian theologian, St. Paul (d. a.d. 69). Paul's letters to various local churches form an extended commentary on Christ as saviour. In one of these letters, that to the Christians in Rome, Paul explained that men and women are made acceptable to God not through any efforts or merits of their own but solely through Christ's death on the Cross which atoned for human sin. Here was the root, in Scripture, of the theology of the Reformation, first in Luther, then in Calvin.

An important feature of Christian humanism was a Pauline renaissance which was strongly evident in France and which gave rise to the evangelical reformist, Jacques Lefèvre d'Étaples (c. 1455–1536), who was in many ways Calvin's guide, especially in his appreciation of the centrality of Scripture. As France's leading exponent of the Pauline movement, Lefèvre moved away from a theology of human good works towards one that placed the emphasis on God's grace for the attainment of salvation.

In 1516 Lefèvre's fellow reformist, Guillaume Briçonnet, was made Bishop of Meaux, east of Paris, and the opportunity arose to turn the idea of reform into practical reality. A campaign was set in motion to create a laity well instructed in Christian doctrine, with the Bible freely available in French. A team of dedicated preachers of reform was recruited, including Calvin's later associate, Guillaume Farel. The eventual collapse of the Meaux experiment exposed the inherent difficulties, especially in the tense 1520s, of the kind of moderate, centrist reformism espoused by Briçonnet and Lefèvre. Traditional Catholicism was inextricably bound up with France's social and political structure and there was fear of the spread of the socially corrosive Lutheran infection from neighbouring Germany. Therefore, even moderate criticism and cautious reformism seemed dangerous and out of place. The University of Paris, known as the Sorbonne, Europe's leading Catholic centre of higher education and the self-appointed watchdog of orthodoxy, in 1521 condemned Lefèvre for unorthodoxy. Meanwhile, to the left of Lefèvre and Briçonnet more radical reformers were attracted by direct action, including the destruction of Catholic images, which only deepened the suspicions of conservatives about what was going on in Meaux. By the mid-1520s the Meaux group had broken up, Lefèvre had fled from the diocese and this hopeful experiment in Catholic diocesan reform had come to an end.

All was not lost for the reformists. They had friends in high places, notably the French king's sister, Marguerite of Angoulême, later Queen of Navarre, whose court at Nérac became a refuge for suspect reformists, including Lefèvre. However, the squeezing out of the liberal Christian humanists meant that during the formative period of Calvin's life moderate options were being reduced and stark choices presented between orthodoxy, assent, and tradition on the one hand and open dissent, protest, and repudiation of authority on the other. It is important to realise that Calvin, a man of uncompromising positions, underwent his education in an increasingly polarized and indeed savage world: the first burnings of French

Protestants took place in the mid-1520s. However, although the middle way represented by Lefèvre was largely closed in the 1520s, it remains the case that John Calvin derived a good deal of his intellectual and spiritual formation from the Christian humanism whose leading French representative was Lefèvre.

3
John Calvin: the early years

John Calvin was not a particularly self-revealing man. In this respect, he shows a marked contrast with Martin Luther whose candid reminiscences about his early years have allowed writers to put together psychological biographies of him, including a picture of running conflict with his father. Despite the attempt of Calvin's most recent – and perhaps best – biographer, William Douwoma, to reconstruct a pattern of tension between John Calvin and his father, Calvin himself was silent about any such friction, as he was in general unforthcoming about the details of his private life.

Calvin was born in the city of Noyon in Picardy in north-eastern France on 10 July 1509. His grandfather had been a bargeman, his father, Gérard Cauvin, or Calvin, a clerk and Church lawyer who married into a local city council family; the Calvins were thus 'upwardly mobile'; for all Calvin's later references to his 'originally obscure and humble condition', he was in fact, as he remained throughout his life, the perfect bourgeois, in a sixteenth-century sense of the word.

Calvin's autobiographical reminiscences are fragmentary, dates are imprecise and there has been some disagreement amongst his biographers as to chronology. However, one very distinct impression does come out clearly from his recollections of his early life – that of steady compliance with parental dictates. Head of a family moving steadily up the ladder of French provincial society, Gérard

Calvin sought out those careers for his sons which were best guaranteed to continue the family's social ascent. For the second son, John, theological study leading to a career in the Church – in which Gérard served as a lay official – seemed an ideal route to prosperity and prestige, and the boy was enrolled as a kind of apprentice cleric.

Calvin began his formal education in his native city and then some time between 1520 and 1523 proceeded, along with youths from a local noble ecclesiastical family, to Paris. There he entered the Collège de la Marche so as to consolidate his Latin in preparation for the University's Arts degree course. For the Arts course proper, Calvin moved on to the Collège Montaigu, run on the lines of an austere monastery. There Calvin's studies were focused on philosophy, according to traditional scholastic approaches. He proceeded through Bachelor of Arts and Master of Arts, but then his course of study, which had been pointing towards an ecclesiastical career, was abruptly switched, by a decision on his father's part, towards a law degree. The explanation for his father's decision was probably a perception, to quote John Calvin's own words, 'that the legal profession commonly raised those who followed it to wealth'. The course of study originally chosen, to advance an ecclesiastical career, was much to the young Calvin's taste. However, in line with a life–long belief in parental authority, Calvin accepted this new turn in his career in simple and loyal obedience: 'Thus it came to pass, that I was . . . put to the study of law. To this purpose I endeavoured faithfully to apply myself, in obedience to the will of my father.'

From some point in or after the mid–1520s, Calvin took up the study of law, first at the University of Orléans, then at the University of Bourges. Part of the value of his new legal studies was to deepen his knowledge of history. At Bourges, he concentrated on the study of the ancient Roman law, then at the height of its influence in the Europe of the High Renaissance, with its reverence for every aspect of the classical world. Through his legal studies, Calvin acquired a legacy of classical historical knowledge which never left him and which he was to employ effectively in his later writings. In addition, the orderly systematization of the Roman law undoubtedly left its mark on Calvin's mind. We see this in his major theological work, the *Institutes of the Christian Religion*, a codified doctrinal synopsis laid out in pre-planned sections – in contrast, for instance, with Martin Luther's vast, sprawling, and frequently unplanned output. However, this system and order that we see in the *Institutes*, and indeed in Calvin's whole life and work, came from a passion for order which lay deep in his personality, fostered not by any one academic subject but by the whole of his education.

In 1531 came another of those abrupt changes of direction that characterized so much of Calvin's life. The death of his father in that year released Calvin to follow his own academic bent and devote himself more single-mindedly to the literary and philosophical studies that he had pursued as a sideline while a law student. While he had, as we have seen, accepted his father's career plans for him, he seems to have regarded Gérard's death as making possible an intellectual homecoming through a divine providential release: 'God, by the secret guidance of his providence, . . . gave a different direction to my course.'

Calvin was now drawn towards critical study of Greek and Roman literature, largely along lines traced by the French humanist Guillaume Budé (1467–1540). His arrival into the fellowship of humanist scholars was marked by the edition he published in 1532 of the Roman writer Seneca's *De Clementia, Concerning Clemency*. This work aligned Calvin with the Erasmian school: although in the actual editorship of the text he disagreed in some details with Erasmus, in undertaking this particular task he was in fact following up an open invitation that Erasmus had issued, in 1529, for someone 'more learned, more felicitous, and with the time at his disposal' to publish a proper edition of the Seneca treatise. In preparing this work for the press, Calvin was laying claim to a career and a reputation as a humanist scholar. However, he had not yet completely abandoned his legal studies and this work of Seneca's dealt with a virtue, proper mercy, that lawyers and judges must possess. Explicit Christian inspiration is largely absent from this, Calvin's first literary study. However, clemency was an important Christian virtue and Seneca a writer widely considered to have been close to Christianity. Thus the *De Clementia* edition certainly established Calvin's credentials as a humanist, but perhaps also suggested an incipient Christian humanist after the fashion of Erasmus and Lefèvre.

In the early to mid-1530s Calvin experienced what he came to call an 'unexpected conversion' for which, in characteristic fashion, he made God responsible, since he believed that God's providence was constantly at work in everyday life. This term conversion may require some explanation in the way Calvin uses it. Many religious

13

figures – John Wesley, for instance – have experienced religious conversion. The word did not necessarily mean for them what it tends to mean for us – the acceptance of new beliefs different from those one has held previously. For many, conversion means the enlivening of beliefs previously held but inert up to the point of conversion. For Calvin, conversion meant both a quickening of piety and acceptance of new beliefs plus rejection of earlier tenets sincerely held: 'Since I was too obstinately devoted to the superstitions of the Papacy, God by an unexpected conversion subdued and brought my mind to a teachable frame, which was more hardened in such matters than might have been expected from one at my early period of life.'

We can read between the lines here some of the human influences underlying this conversion, especially the humanist keynote of revulsion against superstition. However, Calvin himself was convinced that his conversion was the product of a divine intervention in his life – and therefore was inclined (as Luther had been with his conversion) to emphasize the dramatic unexpectedness of an encounter in which God had seized control of him. Undoubtedly, his rejection of popery was abrupt, but it led him into a teachable frame in which a slower and indeed more positive doctrinal reconstruction could take place. It is of course possible that, consciously or not, Calvin's repudiation of the papal Church was precipitated by the fact that his father, long at loggerheads with the ecclesiastical authorities in Noyon, died excommunicated by the same Church. It is also the case that Calvin's period of training in the 1520s and 1530s coincided with the phase of early Reformation history when Christian humanists were forced to make fatal choices over belief. Some of the veteran critics of the abuses, if not of the basic beliefs, of the old Church, such as Erasmus and Lefèvre, abandoned or toned down much of their disgruntlement and chose tradition rather than schism. Calvin – and other erstwhile disciples of Erasmus like the Swiss Reformer Ulrich Zwingli – continued the development of their ideas and chose to proceed along routes of protest and of eventual separation from Rome.

Calvin gives us few clues about the date of his conversion, and it may be that in the sense of a rejection of Rome this was accomplished by 1534 whereas the rebuilding of his beliefs was a more gradual process, coming to fruition in the *Institutes of the Christian Religion* of 1536. Certainly, Calvin's deepening alienation from the Roman

14

Church was far enough advanced by late 1533 for him to be involved, dangerously, in a major scandal pitting the orthodox against the heretics.

Evangelical ideas penetrated into France from Germany in the 1520s and 1530s and were encouraged by the king's sister Marguerite. While French conservative opinion, typified by the Paris university of the Sorbonne, was paranoid about any threat to rigid orthodoxy, various incidents, especially those involving Marguerite, were closely watched as indicators of the current state of the rival religious parties. In autumn 1533 one of Marguerite's associates, the new rector of the Sorbonne, Nicholas Cop, delivered the customary rector's address, which Cop turned into a sermon on Jesus's Eight Beatitudes. The sermon, showing the influence of Erasmus, and also of Luther, called for a thoroughgoing spiritual renewal of the Church. It indicated that reformism had penetrated the citadel of hyper-orthodoxy, the Sorbonne. The sermon was adjudged heretical and Cop fled to escape arrest. It used to be thought – and the view has recently been revived – that Calvin composed Cop's speech. If so, it would show where Calvin stood in autumn 1533: an evangelical reformist highly critical of the deficiencies of the Catholic Church. Associated as he was with Lefèvre's school of reform based on New Testament models, Calvin was doubtless repelled by officialdom's over-reaction to the sermon Cop delivered, while he was also doubtless growing increasingly sceptical about the Catholic Church's ability to reform itself along lines laid down by the Lefèvre-Briçonnet group. Remarks he made a few years later might indicate the view of the Catholic Church he had reached by the beginning of 1534: 'Owing to this supine state of the pastors and this stupidity of the people, every place was filled with pernicious errors, falsehoods and superstition.'

His disenchantment would certainly explain the decisive action Calvin took in the spring of 1534 when he gave up the Church incomes that had been settled on him in Noyon. This same year of decision for Calvin was one of acute polarization between the ever more sharply diverging forms of Christianity in France. Cop's attack on tradition had been less extreme than the Sorbonne authorities took it to be, but less than a twelvemonth after Cop's rectorial address there came a real bombshell in the shape of an unrestrained attack on the Mass, the centre of Catholic worship. Written abuse of the Mass in posters prepared by a committed Protestant was distributed around Paris and one was found in the king's quarters. Though an erratic Catholic, Francis I, as effective president of the Church in France, could hardly ignore this insult to orthodoxy. The poster attacks led to mass arrests; the earlier Cop affair had led to Calvin's departure from Paris for the provinces; now the much more dangerous affair of the posters resulted in his flight, along with other Lutherans, from France to Basel in Switzerland early in 1535. A leading printing centre and a self-governing Free City, Basel was one of the rare islands of tolerance in an embattled and bigoted age: fittingly enough, the aged Erasmus was living out the last months of his life there, but the city also hosted several stars of the German and Swiss Reformations. In Basel Calvin settled down to the kind of work that he always claimed was most congenial to him. Familiar as he was with the current Renaissance debate about the merits of an active versus a studious life, Calvin invariably – though we might say erroneously – saw himself as essentially the backroom theorist, the intellectual resource for others more suited to a life of action in the world: 'Being of a disposition somewhat unpolished and bashful, which led me always to love the shade and retirement, I then began to seek some secluded corner where I might be withdrawn from public view . . . my one great object was to live in seclusion without being known . . . I retired . . . to enjoy in some obscure corner the repose which I had always desired' – and so on, in similar vein.

In Basel, as well as helping with a French translation of the Bible, Calvin began to embark on abstruse and theoretical writing, with a book on *Psychopannychia* (The Soul's Sleep), a work which might well have allowed him 'to live in seclusion without being known'. In Basel too his apparent need for seclusion and anonymity can be seen in his assuming an alias. However, even in his written work Calvin was not the scholar pure and simple, and in the Swiss city he worked on a production specifically intended for the everyday world of events and of power.

The major work on which Calvin began working in Basel, the work which was to emerge less than a year from its commencement as *Institutio Religionis Christianae*, was in every way a practical and public book, with a public purpose. The speed with which the book was composed confirms that it was not a work of pure, leisured scholarship but rather one deeply involved with current events and aimed at the real world. The same practical, rather than theoretical and scholarly, concerns on Calvin's part can be seen in a preface which at around this time he contributed to a French Bible translation, dedicated 'To all Emperors, Kings, Princes'. This characteristically Erasmian and intensely practical appeal to men of power is very much to the fore in the *Institutio*. By presenting a balanced, reasoned, and above all a centrist account of Calvin's maturing convictions, the work set out to nullify the libels, as Calvin saw them, of the Sorbonne and of other religious conservatives in France. This was part of a political strategy to win, or to win back, the favour of the French court and thereby to undo the damage caused by the ill-advised placards against the Mass. Calvin's further public purpose in writing this major work of his was to distance his brand of reformism from the radical, indeed revoluntionary, Anabaptist version of the Reformation that had recently gripped the German city of Münster and which in that year of 1535 had introduced there a totalitarian anarchy of communism and enforced promiscuity. Therefore, motivated by the pressure of current events rather than by abstract speculation, Calvin set out to dissociate his form of Reformation from 'Anabaptists and seditious persons, who, by their perverse ravings and false opinions, were overthrowing not only religion but also all civil order'.

So the *Institutio* was, at least in part, a work of propaganda and persuasion, of public rhetoric, an extended lawyer's plea, concerned with the here-and-now – and this functional orientation dictated a certain speed of composition. At the same time – and there is no real contradiction here – it has been convincingly argued that the *Institutio* had the essentially private aim of establishing what Calvin believed. According to Bouwsma, in 1535 'still an Erasmian, Calvin was probably vague about his beliefs. To clarify these matters, . . . Calvin . . . began . . . to write; . . . he undertook to explore his religious beliefs in . . . the first edition of his *Institutes of the Christian Religion*.' Partly as a result of the Cop affair, Calvin had been converted from popery; partly as a consequence of writing the *Institutio*, he became converted to Calvinism.

Institutes of the Christian Religion is not a very good translation of *Institutio Religionis Christianae*, and something along the lines of *Handbook of Christian Piety* might be preferable. However, *Institutes of the Christian Religion* has been consecrated by centuries of common usage in English and we shall retain it here. The version that Calvin published at Basel in 1536 was influenced in its composition by Martin Luther's recent *Short Catechism* (1529). Indeed, the first

17

edition is a relatively short summary and briefer than the subsequent editions that Calvin polished, revised, expanded and translated into French throughout his career. The work is the central, though not the exclusive, repository of Calvin's theology.

4

The Institutes of the Christian Religion

The *Institutes* contain the essence of Calvin's theology, his science of God – earning him the simple but expressive title sometimes used of him by his disciples, 'the theologian', the student of God. In its opening lines, the book sets out its central purpose, the focus on God who is 'infinite wisdom, justice, goodness, mercy, truth, virtue and life'. The work is also about religion: as its sub-title puts it, 'The Basic Teaching of the Christian Religion'. As such, the book is intended to be moderate and consensual rather than divisive and combative. We can see this if we compare the title of Calvin's work with that of the doctrinal summary by the Swiss reformer Ulrich Zwingli (1484–1531): *A Commentary on True and False Religion* (1525), a title that encapsulates confrontation. In contrast, Calvin in the *Institutes* was setting out not to establish one version of Christianity as better than another but rather to establish a unitive Christian religion which is catholic in the sense that it is common to all true Christians.

As well as being a work about God and about religion, the *Institutes* should be seen as a book about man, about piety and salvation: 'The Basic Teaching of the Christian Religion comprising almost the whole sum of godliness and whatever it is necessary to know on the doctrine of salvation'. This means that the work is not a theology in any speculative or merely academic sense: Calvin is insistent on the limits of human knowledge and reason, especially in

19

such mysterious areas as the nature of the Eucharist. The work is, then, a practical handbook, (*Institutio*, a manual) explaining how man is saved, and aimed at an audience of serious Christians who, like Calvin himself, were anxious about such matters: 'all who are studious of salvation'. However, in contrast to some medieval devotional manuals, the *Institutes* are not a guide to salvific self-help. Salvation comes only from God in Christ, human actions play no part in man's redemption. Man's role is just confidently to trust in God by faith: 'We have fixed all our confidence in God the Father'. Calvin follows Luther in seeing Christian faith partly as assent to certain beliefs but also as faith in the way we use the term to mean trust, confidence. This confidence appeased the pressing anxiety which, as Bouwsma has shown, was a key feature of Calvin's personality; Calvin saw faith as changing a way of life lived 'in suspense'. However, suspense was in fact bound to arise over deduction from assumptions about the nature of God which, for many of Calvin's followers, became central, the doctrine of election and predestination.

More than most other theologians, Calvin saw God as being all-powerful and all-knowing. Some of his most eloquent passages in the *Institutes* reflect his awe at God's majesty, a feeling which he found fully borne out in Scripture. This majestic, omniscient God was in total control of all events, and the fate of every individual, especially in the all-important matters of salvation and damnation, was not only known to God before all time but was also planned and intended by God. In point of fact, all men, being sinners, deserved divine punishment, but God, of His mere mercy, had ordained some – an elect – to eternal life through 'predestination by which God admits some to hope of life and sentences others to eternal death'. The identity of these groups could not be entirely clear to us: 'we cannot know with the certainty of faith who are chosen'.

For many or most of Calvin's contemporaries, if not for us, the quest for personal salvation in an afterlife – or the avoidance of eternal damnation – was a matter of the greatest urgency. Though Calvin claimed that the doctrine of election had the power to console, for many of his followers it set up new cycles of anxious effort as they sought to recognize themselves through their meritorious lives as God's chosen ones.

A possible difficulty that arose from Calvin's conception of God and the doctrine of predestination that flowed from it concerned the authorship of sin. Since Calvin emphasized that God willed and designed all things, it seemed to some of Calvin's opponents that Calvin viewed God as willing the sins by which those He rejected – the reprobate – were damned. From this point of view, the words 'sin only excepted' in Calvin's dictum 'whatever comes to pass (sin only excepted) is from God' might appear illogical – an issue on which Calvin was to be vulnerable during his ministry in Geneva.

In discussing Calvin's most important single work, the *Institutes*, we ought not to be too preoccupied with the concept of predestination, though Calvin himself, and to an even greater extent his followers, tended to emphasize it increasingly in the years after 1536. Calvin's *Institutes* are in fact a comprehensive survey of the whole of Christian doctrine, in which election plays only one part as a necessary corollary of God's sovereignty. In part, the work is, as we have seen, a response to current events: for instance, Calvin dealt with the issues that the Anabaptists of the radical Reformation were raising at that time, such as infant or adult baptism and private or common property. However, as well as being a work of its time, addressing current issues, the *Institutes* form a lasting monument to the school of Christian theology that we may loosely label Augustinian – a school to which Calvin's mentor, Luther, very much belonged. Its characteristics were confidence in God rather than man, and consequent pessimism about man's capacity to earn salvation apart from God in Christ. As the *Institutes* grew in length and depth through Calvin's life, the work turned into a monumental restatement of Augustinian principles and a massively authoritative survey of God, man and Christ, Scripture, faith, hope and charity, the Church and sacraments, justification, civil government, the Christian in society – and so on. In contrast with some of Martin Luther's highly polemical anti-Catholic writings, Calvin generally tried to avoid writing combatively. He does, it is true, take sideswipes at 'Romanists' and 'half-papists' (and also demolishes one fellow-Protestant theologian, the Lutheran Osiander), and he attacks the medieval Catholic scholastic theologians; however, he also cites with approval the medieval monastic leader Bernard of Clairvaux, so that the *Institutes* have at times a quite ecumenical appearance. His other authorities include (of course) St. Augustine, and his humanist learning is on display with his references to Vergil and to classical history. However, his main source is, inevitably, Scripture, in both the Old and New Testaments, all of whose writers, he believed, were 'clerks of the Holy Spirit'. All in all, Calvin's *Institutes* established him, along with Luther, as the intellectual power-house of the Reformation.

5

Geneva

As we have seen, Calvin, despite all his protestations of the love of pure scholarship, was concerned in the *Institutes* with essentially practical questions of religion. This basic practicality was to have ample scope in the active work that Calvin did in the Reformation of the city of Geneva.

Not only did this reticent scholar, as he liked to see himself, embark on an intensely public life of struggle, fame and notoriety, but this deeply patriotic Frenchman was to spend the remainder of his life in exile and after the mid-1530s never saw his beloved France again. Instead, he became part of the large sixteenth-century European population of religious refugees from persecution, many of them found in the cities of Switzerland and its neighbourhood. The *Institutes* completed in a savage burst of hard work, Calvin left Basel for the Italian city-state of Ferrara where a glittering princely court protected religious dissidents under the patronage of a French princess. From Ferrara, Calvin, under an amnesty for heretics, returned briefly to France in 1536 to sort out family affairs, then set out for Strassburg, western Germany's leading Protestant city and a haven for a wide range of religious dissidents. We shall let Calvin himself take up the next stage of the story: 'As the most direct road to Strassburg . . . was shut up by the wars [between France and the Habsburgs], I had resolved to pass quickly by Geneva, without staying longer than a single night in the city.' Calvin went on to

23

relate how a local resident discovered him, and revealed his identity – that of the author of the *Institutes* – to the city's Protestant leader, Guillaume Farel, the former associate of the Lefèvre–Briçonnet reform scheme in Meaux. Entrusted now with the Reformation of Geneva, Farel sought assistance amidst the storms of faction that the recent introduction of Protestantism had awoken in this Savoyard city. Reformation to the Genevans meant the overthrow not only of Catholic ecclesiastical government but also of the rule of its former overlord, the neighbouring duchy of Savoy. A heady sense of revolutionary emancipation made the citizens reluctant to accept constraints, least of all those of disciplinarian Protestantism. Farel badly needed help and, Calvin later recalled, 'detained me at Geneva, not so much by counsel and exhortation, as by a dreadful imprecation, which I felt to be as if God had from heaven laid His mighty hand upon me to arrest me . . . [Farel] strained every nerve to detain me.'

Guillaume Farel was not, perhaps, cut out for the work of a great constructive reformer: what Calvin rightly identified as his 'extraordinary zeal' could so easily turn into what Calvin also called his 'excessive vehemence' and an impulsiveness that was often his undoing. Farel's major contributions to the Genevan Reformation were in piloting through its introduction and in securing Calvin to consolidate it. Yet, defective as he may have been as a long-term builder, Farel clearly excelled as a psychologist, for he knew exactly how to crack the defences of Calvin's self-image as a scholar in retirement from the active world. As Calvin showed in the *Institutes*, the essential characteristic of Christ, the pattern for all Christians, was obedience to the will of the Father. Farel now confronted Calvin with a test of obedience, the kind of test he felt he had passed a couple of years before with his conversion in response to God's will. Nor did Calvin fail this second test of obedience. Once again, divine providence, whose instrument was Farel, was at work at a crossroads in Calvin's life. Indeed, Calvin might even have traced the hand of providence in the military emergency which brought him to Geneva, for God sometimes worked His purposes through war, 'as though He assembled soldiers by the call of a trumpet'.

If war brought Calvin to Geneva, conflict was to be the pattern of his first stay there, and indeed of much of his quarter-century of mission and ministry in the city. Calvin's role in the life of Reformation Geneva was, of course, absolutely decisive. His presence and work there completely transformed the place and turned this some-what introverted and provincial (though fairly sizeable) town into an international centre, the intellectual motor of European Calvinism. And this ascendancy depended on the personal presence of Calvin and of his immediate successors. As Gillian Lewis has shown, after Calvin's death and that of his successor Theodore Beza in 1603, Geneva partly reverted to what it had been before Calvin's arrival there – something of a backwater, with the intellectual leadership of the Calvinist international shifting to England's Cambridge, Holland's Leiden and Germany's Heidelberg. Yet, despite or even because of the fact that Calvin made Geneva the headquarters of Reformed Christianity, his stay there was seldom peaceful. He encountered, as we shall see, bitter opposition from anticlericals, traditionalists, libertarians and localists, and his regime was never a dictatorship. Indeed, Calvin himself recalled that hardly was he established at Geneva when opposition broke out, especially from Anabaptist radicals whose origins lay in nearby Swiss cantons. Faction and opposition mounted against Calvin and Farel, and in May 1538 'I was banished from Geneva'.

Thus Calvin gives us the bare bones of an intriguing story. What exactly had happened? A formidable alliance forced Calvin and Farel out of Geneva, a coalition made up on the one hand of religious radicals who aimed at a toleration that was anathema to Calvin, and on the other hand of anticlericals seeking to maintain individual freedom and the supremacy of Geneva's ruling councils over the ministry. This issue of the authority of the clergy – in a city that had but recently forcibly ejected its ruling bishop – came to a head over the questions of excommunication and a definition of civic faith. Excommunication – the exclusion of individuals from the Eucharist, mostly for moral offences – had social and political as well as purely religious implications. Consequently, the Genevan magistracy tried to insist on having a major voice as to when and how it was pronounced, since it effectively expelled individuals from the local community over which the elected government of Geneva presided. For Calvin, on the other hand, excommunication was the most effective weapon in the Church's disciplinary armoury, to be used judiciously but to be used all the same, and by the Church itself, not by the state, except in a back-up role.

It is true that Calvin had a deep and abiding respect for the legitimate authority of the state, which was appointed by God; as he wrote in the *Institutes*, 'Its function among men is no less than that of bread, water, sun and air; indeed, its place of honour is far more excellent', and he was prepared to 'commit to civil government the duty of rightly establishing religion'. However, the Church also had its appointed sphere; no mere human society, it was made up of those who 'have been chosen in Christ by virtue of the divine goodness before the foundation of the world'. On numerous occasions throughout his career, Calvin's elevated sense of the dignity and autonomy of the Church, its supremacy in spiritual matters, would draw him into conflict with the Genevan magistracy.

Assuming the position of minister of religion, Calvin, with Farel, submitted to the city government a programme for the reformation of the Church, the *Articles on the Organisation of the Church* of January 1537. These were based on the blueprint set out in the *Institutes* and, in particular, Calvin's doctrine of the Church just outlined. Two features of the *Articles* were to cause trouble, both related to the Eucharist and concerning its reception and its withholding. Calvin's whole conception of the Eucharist as the sign of unity between Christ and the Church induced him to emphasize the need for frequent reception of the Sacrament. Since the Eucharist was, like God's grace, a free, unearned gift, there could be no question of worthiness to receive it: for Calvin, that was just the point, that the Eucharist 'would be of no use to us . . . if we were not weak'. However, as part, perhaps, of a trend towards elevating man's role in a merit-oriented view of salvation, the medieval Catholic Church had been tending towards restricting the reception of Holy Communion to those infrequent occasions, usually after confessing their sins and having them absolved, when Christians might be deemed more worthy to receive it. Thus there were deeply embedded popular inhibitions about frequent reception of Holy Communion and Calvin found that his calls for monthly reception, without sacramental confession and absolution, awoke deep misgivings in people who took the Eucharist seriously.

Calvin did not, of course, in any way deprecate the sacrament of Holy Communion, one of the two sacraments (along with Baptism) that he retained in the Church from Catholicism's total of seven. He believed that while Christians ought, as a pledge to Christ, to receive this sacrament fairly often, *only* Christians ought to receive it. These Christians were identified, as the *Institutes* had indicated they would be, in terms of their orthodox faith and the orderly virtue of their private lives. Orthodoxy – Calvin insisted that Christians should share only one faith – was defined in terms of a *Confession of Faith* drawn up by Calvin and subscribed by all.

Here Calvin was introducing nothing less than an eucharistic revolution in Geneva. Whereas the medieval Catholic Church recently swept away in Geneva had tended to admit virtually all baptized adults infrequently to Holy Communion, Calvin proposed the frequent reception of the Sacrament by a morally and credally tested élite. Though this arrangement might well 'build up' the Church, it threatened to divide and disrupt the community. A clash between Calvin and Farel and the representative government of this community was inevitable. In Easter week 1538 conflict came to a head over a relatively minor issue concerning what sort of bread was to be used in the Eucharist and, amidst crowd disorders directed against Calvin, the Genevan government brutally resolved matters by ordering Calvin and Farel to leave the city almost immediately. The question of what sort of bread to use in Communion was not in itself important – not to Calvin anyway, since he pursued a consistent policy of indifference in these external matters. However, the question brought into focus, as trivial matters often do, more complex and deep-seated problems: whether the Genevan Reformation should take its tone from Calvin or from already established Swiss models, and whether the council or Calvin should have the final say in ecclesiastical matters. Always convinced of his own rightness, Calvin never learned to give way – to face defeat, that is – on questions of his or the Church's authority. The leading lights of Swiss Protestantism, in reviewing the Genevan crisis, apportioned the blame for the breakdown equally between Calvin and the 'undisciplined people' of Geneva. In defence of Calvin, it might be said that he could have accepted the council's supremacy in this matter only at the cost of becoming a tame and probably despised corporation chaplain in a disagreeable and contentious market town. Surely there was a better future for this leading theologian of the Reformation. A great city beckoned, a great cosmpolitan intellectual centre where for Calvin thankless tasks made way for congenial work, shame and opposition for honour and co-operation, provincial obscurity for international repute.

27

6

Strassburg

'Then afterwards I was expelled from this town [of Geneva] and went away to Strassburg, and when I had lived there some time I was called back hither.' Thus Calvin, in his farewell address to the Geneva councillors in 1564, laconically recalled his stay in Strassburg between 1538 and 1541. He makes his Strassburg period appear a brief interlude only, whereas in fact it formed a crucial period in his life. In the first place, he came under the decisive influence of Protestant Strassburg's leading pastor, Martin Bucer or Butzer (1491–1551). Bucer had a major personal impact on Calvin's views, including his view of the Church and of Christian society. Secondly, as we shall see, Calvin produced major writings while at Strassburg. Thirdly, Calvin, from his base at Strassburg, enhanced his status as a leading international Protestant figure. Finally, on the personal front, Calvin married while at Strassburg.

In the course of the 1520s, Strassburg, partly under pressure from its lower classes, went over to the Reformation. The dominant doctrine showed important differences from the Protestantism upheld by Martin Luther at Wittenberg. Strassburg was also a relatively open city in terms of beliefs – a magnet for diverse radicals – and in that respect quite different from the uniform model that Calvin had in mind for his ideal Reformation city. Strassburg had been identified as a kind of city of God by the radical Anabaptist prophet Melchior Hoffman (d. 1543) and the city was for a time a refuge for Anabaptist dissidents, advocates of a far-reaching and radical Reformation of the Church and society. Calvin had dealings with the Strassburg Anabaptists and married the widow of one of them.

After leaving Geneva in May 1538, Calvin was inclined to resume his scholarly career in Basel. However, Martin Bucer wanted him for Strassburg, and was shrewd enough to use Farel's technique of presenting an invitation in the guise of an irresistible divine command: 'Do not think', Bucer wrote to Calvin, 'that you can leave the ministry even for a short time without offending God, if another ministry is offered you'. Three years later, this perception of divine mandate, which brought Calvin to Strassburg, would take him from that place and back to Geneva. In the meantime, though, there was important work to be done at Strassburg which, as the most important German Protestant city nearest to France, was host to a sizeable French *émigré* Protestant community of up to 500. Calvin's principal role at Strassburg was to provide pastoral ministry for this Francophone community. In addition, he played a leading part in international discussions with Catholic representatives and also developed his reputation as an author. The *Institutes* were considerably expanded for publication in 1539, with the addition of six new chapters, including one on predestination, and the existing material enlarged. Calvin partly intended the *Institutes* as background reading for the detailed, or exegetical, reading of passages of Scripture, and he showed how this exegesis was to be carried out in his *Commentaries on the Epistle of Paul to the Romans* which he published in March 1540.

Based on up-to-date textual research and sound Greek texts, the *Commentaries on Romans* were both Calvin's acknowledgement of the Pauline roots of French Christian humanism and also his own salute to one of the great monuments of the Reformation, since the Epistle of St Paul was the source for Martin Luther's evangelical doctrine of the sufficiency of God's free grace, without human involvement, in the attainment of salvation. In addition to this pivotal work, opening up a quarter century's continuous work in scriptural commentary, Calvin also – and most significantly – kept open his links to Geneva with a controversial publication in the autumn of 1539, the *Reply to Sadoleto*.

Cardinal Jacopo Sadoleto (1477–1547), one of a group of reform-minded but essentially Catholic prelates, had written an open letter to the Genevans attempting to persuade them to return to their historical Catholic faith. The Genevan city government, still committed to Reformation and looking for a controversialist to answer Sadoleto, approached Calvin, who composed a hastily written polemical masterpiece. In the *Reply to Sadoleto*, the former law student Calvin, though with considerable courtesy to his opponent, dealt point by point with the Catholic attack on the Reformation. It was deeply significant for Calvin's immediate future that he should have taken it upon himself to rebut Sadoleto's message to Geneva and he clearly felt he still had a pastoral responsibility towards the city: 'I am *at present* [my emphasis] relieved of the charge of the Church of Geneva . . . but God, when he gave it me in charge . . . bound me to be faithful to it for ever . . . I cannot cast off that charge any more than that of my own soul.'

Calvin, then, still felt that he was very much minister to Geneva and that God, who did not go back on His decisions, had given him a charge in trust which mere human machinations could not cancel. Eventually, these considerations would bring about Calvin's return to Geneva when the time was right. In the meantime, this work, occasioned by Genevan concerns, had, as did this stage of Calvin's career, a European interest, for the booklet made a major contribution to the mounting Catholic-Protestant clash, a collision in which Calvin and his followers were to play the part of shock-troops – the more so as the Lutheran movement began to lose some of its impetus.

A polemical, not to say a combative, approach also characterizes another work from this fruitful Strassburg period, the *Short Treatise on the Holy Supper of the Lord Jesus Christ* (1540), in which Calvin spent some time violently attacking the Catholic doctrine of the Mass. The dialectical vehemence may be distasteful to us today, but it is refreshing that, in an age when so many theologians were prepared to try to define or even explain the Eucharist minutely, Calvin in this work was content to leave it ultimately as a mystery beyond human ken: 'the communion which we have with the body of Christ is a thing incomprehensible'. Though there is some attempt at definition, Calvin, in the *Treatise on the Supper*, concentrates on practical questions of the reception of the Eucharist.

Written first in French, the *Treatise on the Supper* is one of those works which have established Calvin's lasting reputation as one of the foremost architects of the literary French language and prose style. Along with other titles in Calvin's Strassburg corpus of writings, this work – which was warmly welcomed by Luther – confirmed his standing as the leading intellectual light of the Reformation. As such, he was involved in Catholic–Protestant dialogues in a number of German cities. However, one particular city was calling him back to itself.

7

Return to Geneva

During Calvin's absence, the situation in Geneva deteriorated
rapidly. The local Church was split and this religious schism was
paralleled by political discord, which contemporaries regarded not
as healthy opposition but as faction, harmful to the urban community which was viewed as, ideally, an united body politic. Early
in 1540, accidental deaths, judicial executions and political banish-
ments drastically reduced the numbers of the councillors opposed to
Calvin, and the pro-Calvin lobby moved into power. Serious
attempts to get Calvin back began in September 1540, with a
Genevan embassy to Strassburg and a tearful interview with the
reformer.

It is tempting for us, with hindsight, to see Calvin's spell away
from Geneva as a kind of sabbatical leave and his return as inevitable.
After all, he had more than kept up his contacts with the city and in
the *Reply to Sadoleto* he had written as if he were Geneva's guardian at
a distance. However, the prospect of returning to Geneva filled
Calvin with deep repugnance which we cannot regard as merely
rhetorical; he spoke, for instance, of the 'grief, tears, great anxiety
and distress' with which he contemplated return. Yet central to
Calvin's thinking was the theme of conquest over personal incli-
nations. Although, as his *Reply to Sadoleto* showed, Calvin saw
himself essentially as Geneva's pastor in temporary exile, he was, we
may believe, genuinely averse to returning, and, what is more, had

to see himself as being reluctant to return. Calvin was influenced by examples of Old Testament prophets who were, typically much against their will, seized upon by God and made His vessels at the cost of great suffering. God's direct command had prompted Calvin's conversion leading to deprivation and exile. Subsequently, God's order, delivered through human mouthpieces, had established Calvin first in Geneva, then in Strassburg; God's mandate was now to bring him back to Geneva. There was, once again, a human intermediary, Bucer. Calvin reverenced Bucer as a father-figure: 'do all those things', he wrote to Bucer in 1541, 'that a father may do to his son'. Effectively, Calvin left the decision on his return in Bucer's hands, and Bucer recommended that he go back. But Calvin was convinced that the real decision was God's; he had made up his mind, he said, 'never again to enter on any ecclesiastical charge whatever unless the Lord should call me to it by a clear and manifest call. . . . I am prepared to follow entirely the Lord's calling.'

Even a clear and manifest call sometimes has to be negotiated, and Calvin was a cautious and prudent man who needed a detailed specification of the terms on which he was to return to Geneva. Above all, he wanted a much clearer statement and acceptance of his authority than had existed in 1536–8. He also needed, and got, a release from Strassburg. Some suave correspondence took place with the Genevan authorities – Calvin could be a polished diplomat when he wanted or needed to be. Satisfactory arrangements were worked out for accommodation, salary, grain and wine, for even great reformers, and their families, have to live. Finally, Calvin returned to Geneva in September 1541. The city was to have its second, more protracted and much more intensive experience of being taken in hand.

In the negotiations leading up to Calvin's return to Geneva, he insisted on being given a reasonably free hand and on the Genevans' acceptance of his plans for moral and doctrinal discipline. At this fourth crossroads in his life, he saw himself, once again, as simply an instrument of divine providence. He was also convinced of his own rightness and essentially unrepentant about his part in the events leading to his earlier exile. He seems, on the whole, to have regarded the Strassburg period as an interlude, and simply resumed preaching where he had left off in 1538. Yet the interlude was useful from his point of view since his time away from Geneva had allowed the situation there to be redrawn in his favour. He returned in a mood of discreet triumph, and his personal ascendancy was emphasized by Farel's acceptance of a ministry at Neuchâtel in French-speaking Switzerland.

Even so, Calvin's role in Genevan life was still construed by the city's political authorities in terms of service. The council minutes, noting his return, recorded that 'he offered himself to be always the servant of Geneva'. Calvin, indeed, especially in the earlier years of his second Genevan ministry, assumed the role of an agent of the city government, carrying out tasks which we might find unusual in a minister of religion. For instance, by 1543 he had helped draft a new civic constitution, work in which his training in law came in useful. Other secular work in which Calvin was involved as 'the servant of Geneva' included a foreign policy review, in 1543–4, of the city's relations with its ally, the Swiss city-state of Bern.

So Calvin entered once more upon his Genevan ministry, performing functions that were both useful and subservient: 'the servant of Geneva'. However, in matters concerning the Church he was a masterful servant. From about the mid-1540s to the mid-1550s Calvin and the Genevan political authorities entered a phase of intense competition. The city rulers, like their opposite numbers in German and Swiss Protestant cities in the 1520s and 30s, had, through the process of Reformation, won major victories over urban clergies. In German cities such as Nuremberg and and Swiss cities such as Zürich, local councils took over the administration of education and poor relief, appointed clerics, and, in general, vastly expanded their competence and supervision of local life. Geneva was certainly no exception to this pattern, and, as its historian, E. William Monter, puts it, the city's rulers did everything 'from approving catechisms to reproving peasants'. Geneva's magistrates were, like those of the German and Swiss Protestant cities, overwhelmingly committed to the Reformation, but they had gained considerable power at the expense of the clergy and were not prepared to renounce any of that authority to a new breed of clerics with John Calvin at their head. Thus a long-running clash occurred between Calvin and the magistracy over the balance of power and authority between state and Church, for Calvin had no intention of making the Church simply a department of the all-powerful state.

In Calvin's view, the Church was God's instrument, and its ministers God's anointed ones. Geneva, with Calvin's help, acquired a new political constitution by 1543, but even before that the Genevan Church had its own constitution, Calvin's *Ecclesiastical Ordinances* of 1541. In preparing this Church constitution, Calvin intended to reconstruct what he saw as the authentic model of the Church's organization in its earliest apostolic period immediately following the life of Christ and before the Church became tarnished with accretions having only human authority. Calvin, then, intended to put into effect a divine blueprint of the Church based on evidence derived from the New Testament. Using this information, Calvin organized the ministry in the four New Testament offices. These were: pastors, who administered the sacraments and preached; doctors, who gave instruction in Christian doctrine; lay elders, who administered moral discipline; and lay deacons, who organized poor relief. A hallmark of the system was its relative autonomy and independence from the civil authority. However, that spirit of independence soon strained relations between ministry and magistracy in Geneva, in particular over the question of the responsibility of the key element in the ministry, the pastorate, towards the government, and over the social and political implications of the imposition of Church discipline, especially through excommunication.

In autumn 1541 Calvin's draft of the *Ordinances* was dragged through Geneva's complex hierarchy of governing councils and subjected to extensive revision. In insisting upon these revisions, the civil magistrates were, in all probability, not simply airing their views on the substantive issues, but also making a more general claim in principle to a sovereignty only recently achieved over religious matters. With regard to the specific and vexed question of the relationship of the pastors to the city government, pastors, it was decided, were to be chosen by their ministerial colleagues but confirmed by the government, and they were then to swear a loyalty oath to Geneva, its government and its laws; further, if convicted of a serious fault, a pastor was to be deposed and otherwise punished by the civil authorities. As for moral discipline of Church members and citizens – they were the same thing – Calvin himself was anxious to bring the secular government fully into this vital function of the Church. The elders, who joined with the pastors to form the disciplinary body known as the Consistory, were drawn from the lay government and the chairman was a sort of consul known as the *syndic*. Geneva's lay rulers maintained steady pressure to uphold the state's jurisdiction over that of the Consistory, especially with regard to the essentially social sanction of excommunication.

Over the obligations of pastors towards the state, the state's oversight of pastors, and the relative roles of the clergy and the civil government in the process of excommunication, there was enormous potential for recurrent discord. This discord was indeed present in the very process of hammering out the *Ordinances*. During that process, the councillors' guarded attitude was clearly expressed in the concluding clause they insisted on having inserted in the *Ordinances* so as to protect their hard-won ecclesiastical authority from Calvin and the pastors: 'These arrangements do not mean that the pastors have any civil jurisdiction.' From the councillors' point of view, though, they themselves were to exercise an ecclesiastical jurisdiction.

Ominously, then, the protracted negotiations leading to the adoption of the *Ordinances* pointed to a future of disagreement and tension, especially in the light of Calvin's strongly held views on the dignity and autonomy of the Church. Disagreement might mean a constant process of seeking adjustments in the power relationship, or it could amount to serious breakdowns of relations between Church and state. Indeed, collisions, of varying levels of seriousness, arose because of the very mingling of roles written into the 1541 *Ecclesiastical Ordinances*. Church–state conflicts are less likely to occur in systems in which the Church and the state each keeps as much as possible to a clearly defined role, a secular one for the state, a spiritual one for the Church. This specialization of functions did not exist, and was not intended to exist, in Calvin's Geneva. Close state involvement in religion – in any case inevitable in the sixteenth century – was built into the *Ordinances*, especially in the way the council was involved in consistorial discipline. On the other hand, Calvin, as we have seen, operated as a state servant; he had strong political views and was sure to be caught up in secular politics whenever the interests of the Church, however broadly defined, were concerned.

8

The years of opposition

The opposition that Calvin faced in Geneva was at its most intense in a period of about ten years between the mid-1540s and the establishment of his authority on a firmer basis from around the mid-1550s. There were varied strands of opposition, though they tended to coalesce. The principal strands were: first, resistance to Calvin's vision of a disciplined, godly society whose moral constraints would apply to everyone, including Geneva's leading families; second, nativist hatred of foreigners aimed against Calvin, his fellow Frenchmen and other outsiders attracted to this increasingly magnetic city for European Protestants; third, hostility to Calvin's aim of converting Geneva into an unanimous society with a single religious belief; and, fourth, the whole protracted question of the secular government's jurisdiction.

From about the mid-1540s, the potential for Church–state discord which was implied in the dispute over the passage of the *Ordinances* at the beginning of the decade became activated. At the same time, Calvin became increasingly vulnerable to attack from the local populace over the whole question of moral discipline and the rights of the individual. Questions of personal freedom apart, Calvin's vision of the godly society disrupted an ancient popular culture and suppressed much harmless traditional pleasure-seeking. Professor Elton captures with characteristic vividness the atmosphere of Calvin's Geneva as a moral autocracy in which an 'easy-going, dissolute' city became the 'grim, solid, elevated community of psalm-singing church-goers'. Indeed, as we shall see, such a change in Geneva's collective personality really did take place, but initially the Calvinist cultural revolution encountered stiff, and surely understandable, resistance. After all, here was a regime that, overnight, laid down rules for the style of women's hats, investigated the insides of tankards and saucepans in homes, prosecuted a man who owned a currently popular novel, punished three youths who had consumed 36 pâtés, disciplined a barber for shaving a priest in Catholic style, censured a woman for praying for her late husband's soul – and so on. Subversive words were certainly forbidden, and indeed something of Calvin's new vulnerability after the mid-1540s is suggested by the prosecution of a man reported to have claimed that French immigration was putting up prices. In 1546 came a whole battery of new authoritarian legislation: stage plays were banned, only certain approved names were to be given to infants in baptism and, in one of the best-known incidents in Calvin's ill-judged social disciplinarianism, the taverns were closed and replaced by the uplifting but short-lived *Abbayes* where bibles provided the only entertainment.

This was all too much, too far, too fast: the new system awoke widespread but unfocused popular antipathy which fused with powerful upper-class resistance to produce the most serious crisis in Calvin's second Geneva ministry. Early stirrings of serious opposition came in 1546 with the trial of one Pierre Ameaux. Ameaux was a playing-card manufacturer – an endangered species in Calvin's strait-laced Geneva – who had quarrelled with Calvin over his divorce and who subsequently tried to get even with the reformer by attacking him for false teaching. Calvin successfully demanded from the magistrates a humiliating sentence for Ameaux. Nevertheless, it was a pointer towards future conflict that the councillors were strongly inclined to remit the card-maker's sentence and Calvin had to use blackmail in the form of a threat to cease preaching in order to have the full humiliating punishment exacted.

All the same, this was a victory and showed that in encounters over discipline Calvin could still sway the magistracy. However, the Ameaux case marked the end of a period, since 1541, during which Calvin's leadership had been more or less generally accepted. As 1546 progressed, Calvin ran into stiffer opposition – not from a disgruntled local small businessman but from an interlocked and intermarried oligarchy of civic patricians. Calvin despised these men, not only for what he saw as their disordered lives but also for their inflated social pretensions: this Parisian educated cosmopolite looked down upon the provincial big-wigs now about to gang up on him. In particular, he dismissed their leader, Ami Perrin, as 'our comic Caesar'. But although the dismissive phrase identified Perrin's probable dictatorial ambitions, Calvin was mistaken to underestimate the new libertarian opposition and its leader, for Perrin was to be a formidable antagonist: a remarkable political survivor, a resourceful military commander, a would-be international diplomat, and above all a gifted and well-connected party leader.

Perrin built up his libertarian, laicist, xenophobic political movement largely on the basis of his own extensive family connections with Geneva's leading clans, and emphasized the strong local appeal of a grouping which took the name *enfants de Genève*, 'Geneva lads'. Perrin had serious political ambitions and it is entirely possible that he aimed at a personal dictatorship to supplant Geneva's creaking medieval constitution. If that were the case, collision between him and Calvin would be unavoidable, even though he had been the leading light in the moves to recall Calvin in 1540–1. He was in fact drawn into conflict with Calvin – this was the immediate cause, at least – over an alleged moral offence of dancing at a society wedding, for which offence he was briefly imprisoned. Others close to Perrin – his wife and his father-in-law, François Favre – were feeling the lash of consistorial discipline at around this time. Indeed, one has an unmistakeable sense of the outrage felt by these old-established Genevan families at being caught up, along with mere commoners, in the tightening disciplinarian net created by an outsider who had become too big for his boots. Calvin's discipline was indeed being intensified at this time – the taverns were shut down in 1546 and the theatre suppressed. In this initial clash, however, Perrin came to terms with Calvin over the wider moral question and the authority that the Consistory exercised over all Genevans.

This was no more than a temporary truce. The year 1547 saw threats of violence aimed against Calvin and his ministerial colleagues, council elections going badly against Calvin's partisans and the real threat of a second, and surely final, departure of Calvin from Geneva. In 1548 Ami Perrin secured the key military position of captain-general and for the next five years Calvin would have to co-exist with Perrin and a city government hostile and suspicious towards him. In fact, the anti-Calvinist opposition's power rose to its highest point in 1552, Perrin then becoming both civic and military leader and his relatives and associates being placed in key governmental positions. Magistrates once again challenged the ministers over the old issue of control over excommunication. Yet, in many ways unexpectedly, by the end of 1555 Calvin had won an outright victory over the Perrinists.

9

The road to victory

How did Calvin's eventual victory over his opponents in Geneva
come about? For one thing, the very strength of Perrin's position and
that of his ramified political connections caused evident unease over a
monopoly of power and patronage in the hands of one particular
faction. In response to this unease and partly also as a result of the
enfranchisement of pro-Calvin French expatriates, council elections
in February 1555 led to landslide victories for Calvin's partisans.
These results seem to have induced Perrin to attempt a coup, but the
resultant messy street fighting cast this man of action in the character
of a discredited and ineffective man of violence. Perrin's speedy
departure for Bern in the summer was followed by a blood-letting of
his followers.

As we shall see, this sensational political turnabout in 1555 was
preceded and made possible by slower-working demographic,
cultural and educational trends. But in seeking to explain Calvin's
apparently sudden victory in that year we need also to be aware that
in the years between 1546 and 1555, despite apparent reverses,
Calvin's underlying position was in fact quietly and steadily
improving.

In the early 1550s in particular, Calvin encountered and overcame
a series of challenges, especially to his doctrinal views and in
vanquishing a procession of opponents put himself in what had
become by 1555 a strongly entrenched position. None of his

individual opponents of those years was as formidable as was Ami Perrin, placed as he was in the centre of a web of Genevan patronal and kinship relationships. Yet the string of victories that Calvin won over assorted foes eventually gave him a secure base from which to confront Perrin and his allies in 1555. In part, the triumph that Calvin secured in 1555 came about because of the reputation he built up, in a series of show trials, as the guardian of public morality, of theological orthodoxy, and of Reformation principles. The banishment in December 1551 of Jerome Bolsec, who had challenged Calvin's doctrine of predestination, established Calvin's theology as the faith of Geneva, a victory sealed by the suppression of a second anti-predestinarian, Jean Troillet, in 1552. Early in 1553 the dismissal of a dissident cleric, Philippe de Ecclesia, confirmed Calvin's control over the local clergy.

This run of victories in the field of dogma was clinched in the great theological *cause célèbre* of Calvin's career, the battle with Michael Servetus in 1553. Like Jerome Bolsec, Michael Servetus (Miguel Servedo) was a medical doctor. A Spaniard, he was deeply and variously learned as a classicist, mathematics lecturer and creative medical writer. He had also had intermittent written contact with Calvin. When it came to theology, the two could not have differed more markedly. Whereas for Calvin the orthodox doctrine of the three-in-one nature of God as a Trinity of Persons was central, Servetus insistently denied this cornerstone of Trinitarian Christianity, along with the practice of infant baptism, generally considered a vital cement between Church and society.

Fatally, Servetus, a dissident theologian on the run, with a history of aliases and narrow escapes, arrived in Geneva in the summer of 1553 and was promptly arrested at Calvin's behest. Calvin's central role in the prosecution of Servetus was a key factor in the turning of the tide in his favour and against his Genevan opponents in the mid-1550s. At issue here were the central teachings of the Christian Church – doctrines on which, as the current saying went, 'the church stood or fell' – and Calvin was to ride to their defence. An ill-advised, last-ditch attempt by Ami Perrin to save Servetus collapsed, and Perrin had in the end to comply with a death sentence by burning which was carried out against Servetus late in October 1553.

It is true that Calvin was unsuccessful in his plea that Servetus be hanged rather than burned. However, the victory against the Spanish dissident was very much his. Indeed, Servetus was the unwitting victim of a power struggle between Calvin and his Genevan opponents in which, as Bouwsma writes, 'each side needed to demonstrate its zeal for orthodoxy'. In addition, the Servetus case confirmed the outcome of the earlier heresy trials and underlined Calvin's view that only one form of religion could exist in a state, along with his insistence that the political authorities had the duty to suppress religious dissent 'so that idolatry, sacrilege of the name of God, blasphemies against His truth and other public offences against religion may not emerge and may not be disseminated'. Calvin stoutly defended this view of the closed society against the contemporary apostle of religious toleration, Sebastian Castellio, and the fact that the rulers of Geneva were in harmony with his views underlined the victory of his vision of the unanimous community. The later case of the Italian anti-Trinitarian, Valentino Gentile, whose death sentence was repealed, confirmed Calvin's role as defender of the faith of Geneva. Thus the outcome of these contests was a victory for him not because he was defending disputed points of his own theology but because he occupied the morally impregnable role of guardian of a traditional Christian corpus of belief. Above all, Michael Servetus helped to make Geneva Calvin's Geneva.

Largely as a result of the doctrinal trials, from the middle of the 1550s Calvin's position in Geneva improved markedly. He was never, though, to attain the position of dictator and it is possible that his strength rested on his setting up an alternative to Perrin's ambitions in that direction. The sentencing of Servetus, when Calvin's request for a less savage punishment was turned down, provides an apt illustration of the limits of his powers. Even at the height of his ascendancy in the city, around 1560, requests that he made over eucharistic procedures and over the disciplining of individuals were rejected by the city government. For all that, there is no doubt that 1555 marked a watershed in his position at Geneva, his authority being so much more firmly secured after that date.

Alongside the string of theological vindications that established his moral and political position, long-term social, demographic, cultural and educational changes in Geneva had also been working steadily to bolster Calvin's leadership of the city. One such change was dramatically visible: the gallicization and internationalization of the city. Speaking a sub-French dialect, Geneva was a natural centre, just outside the French border, for France's Reformed community, a Protestant community itself becoming ever more Calvinist in character. The French refugees brought some wealth to Geneva, and fees for the conferment of citizenship on them made a substantial contribution to the civic budget. However, their very presence was, of course, ineluctably changing the whole character of Geneva and also consolidating Calvin's position there. The waning anti-Calvinist opposition hoisted its flag of nativism and nostalgia for a pre-Calvin Geneva for the last time in the riot in which Perrin, disastrously for him, was implicated in May 1555.

Less visible than the peaceful invasion of Geneva by French and other foreign Calvinist refugees was a slow educational and cultural revolution in the city which was eventually to create a largely Calvinistic population, giving the future to Calvin and his successors. The educational transformation of Geneva in fact created a generation gap. By 1555, the *enfants de Genève* were no longer, if they had ever been, 'lads', and the places they lost in 1555 in Geneva's parliamentary body, the Two Hundred, were filled, significantly, with young men, supporters of Calvin. The impression of an age-gap isolating a pre-Calvin older generation is confirmed by the discovery in 1557 of five men – five old men, survivors from the period before Calvin's arrival – who had to be given a compulsory crash-course in Calvinist dogmatics. From about that year onwards – sixteen years after Calvin's second arrival in Geneva – it could be assumed that all Sunday-school educated Genevans of adult years had been exposed to a lengthy course – truly an indoctrination – in Christian doctrine according to John Calvin. Indeed, consciously or otherwise, Calvin had made sure of this outcome right from the earliest months of his second Genevan ministry, through the prompt composition of an essential teaching tool, a school catechism.

We can only guess at the influence of Calvin's educational programme for training young people in his doctrines. Many must have baulked and others must have remained completely untouched. However, it is a reasonable speculation that his school and catechism curriculum gave him a certain constituency of native Genevan supporters, alongside his faithful foreign immigrants. Indeed, the moral effects of Calvin's didactic transformation were clearly visible. Elton's 'easy-going', 'dissolute' city was no more, and one visitor even noticed a major shift in the city's collective personality: from being 'carefree', the citizens had been made 'a good deal more withdrawn' by 'the Reformation of religion'. This alteration in the

Genevans' collective character, and the consequent existence of genuine support for Calvin and his ideals, within elements, at least, of the Genevan population, may help to explain a mystery of Calvin's Geneva: how this under-policed city came eventually to accept an iron discipline, a discipline that had been widely rejected in the years before Calvin's school training system was producing its gradual results. Eventually, the Calvinist discipline became part of a social self-discipline as a result of an intense educational programme. The political results of this programme are to be seen in the dramatic improvement in Calvin's fortunes from the mid-1550s as his generation began to move into adulthood and as some of them took their first steps on the ladder of Genevan politics. One indicator was a spontaneous mass petition of autumn 1553 rebutting the libertarians' claim to speak for the people of Geneva. This was followed by the electoral landslide of 1555 and, following it, the entry into the Council of Two Hundred of 22 of Calvin's young men.

There may even have been some dimension of social class in the collision between the growing moral puritanism of at least sections of Geneva's common people and the old-fashioned loose living of the libertarian elite. There may also have been a link between on the one hand Calvinism and republicanism and, on the other, Perrinism, oligarchy and even hints of dictatorship. This may appear strange, since Calvin is often regarded as the dictator of Geneva, but up until 1555 the likely candidate for the role of dicator was Ami Perrin. The Perrinist government of the early 1550s was a narrow oligarchy which provoked vocal resentment in this jealously republican city at the prospect of rule by a single dynasty which would lead Geneva into slavery. The Perrinist riot of 16 May 1555 had unmistakeable undertones of an attempted *putsch* by a would-be dictator. Thus, by 1555 it was the Calvinists and Calvin, with his unassuming title of 'moderator of the Genevan company of pastors', who had come to appear in the guise of defenders of republican liberty and equal citizenship. The retreat from the prospect of military coup to the traditions of the civilian republic was marked, and the flight of the Perrinists was commemorated with a council resolution that 'no one speak of making any militia commanders. . . . As befits a good republic, everyone will be simply a citizen.' Traces of Calvin's hatred of all things military can be detected here, along with retrospective references to Perrin's apparent ambition for a military-style autocracy. Traditional Genevan republicanism and Calvinism now came together, and Calvin became spokesman for an ideology of the common good which was an essential part of the outlook of early-modern European cities: no faction, no self-interest, but only the welfare of the whole. As a council resolution put it: 'May everyone keep his obligations . . . to the city which we have promised to serve in adversity and prosperity, so that each man many continue his calling and try neither to withdraw nor to intrigue.'

10
Calvin's leadership: foreign policy

In the years following 1555, the image of the outsider fell away from Calvin and he was finally made a citizen of Geneva in 1559. He had become a spokesman for civic republican values and also for policies that put Geneva's interests first. The Perrinists' projection of themselves as *enfants de Genève* was muddied by the fact that they were oriented towards the Swiss city of Bern: they were great admirers of the Bernese way of doing things, and especially the way Bern managed to keep its clerics in a subordinate role. Significantly, when Perrin and his allies fled, they made for Bern. Now, an alliance of some kind with Protestant Bern was certainly necessary to mid-sixteenth-century Geneva, but Bern was a relatively large and ambitious Swiss city-state, and for Geneva the Bernese alliance, especially the *Combourgeoisie* or civic twinning, was potentially suffocating. Calvin endorsed an alliance with Bern on the best terms for Geneva, but tried to maintain the right degree of diffidence towards the Swiss city and was vigilant over any threat from Bern to Geneva's independence. Meanwhile, the reputation of the Perrinists as Genevan patriots was exploded once and for all in 1563 when Perrinist exiles conspired with Savoy against Genevan independence.

Not only did Calvin thus stand for a free and republican Geneva; he also gave his adopted city a gratifying identity, that of a chosen people. The source was his doctrine of election. God, Calvin

47

explained, had elected the people of Geneva as His chosen people, just as He had the Israelites of old. This choice was not for anything they were or did: God's immutable choices were not made in response to human merit. Therefore, it was possible for the Genevans, like the Israelites, to be both 'perverse and wicked' and a people to whom 'God will give . . . His blessing as a commonwealth humiliated before Him.' Geneva as a community and Church was in a kind of contractual or covenanted relationship with God, and 'If we want to preserve our present condition, we must not dishonour the seat into which He has put us, for He has said that He will honour those who honour Him and will cast down those who scorn Him . . . take courage and fortify yourselves, for God will use this church and will uphold it; I assure you that He will preserve it.'

This calm assurance was all the more necessary given an international and regional situation that grew more menacing for Geneva in the 1550s. Like Israel in the Old Testament, Geneva was girt about with enemies. Threats to the republic's security or even its continued independent existence came from Savoy and from France. The city's former effective sovereign power, the duchy of Savoy, had controlled the vital Genevan hinterland up to 1536 and Savoyard territory had come virtually up to the walls of Geneva. Savoy was an inflexibly Catholic state and the prerequisite for the survival of both the Genevan Reformation and the Genevan republic was freedom from Savoyard control. From the 1550s onwards, Savoy, under its modernizing ruler duke Emmanuel Philibert, was evolving as an absolutist, expansionist, military state. It was firmly within the diplomatic orbit of the all-powerful Habsburgs of Spain and Austria, and would emerge as a political and military mainstay of the Catholic revival known as the Counter-Reformation. Clearly, this powerful Catholic autocracy, the complete antithesis of Geneva's Protestant bourgeois republic, posed a threat to the city, and although during Calvin's time in Geneva Savoyard aggression was held at bay, in 1567 the republic once more lost its hinterland territory to the duchy.

A further threat to Geneva came from France. Admittedly, this danger was one that the Genevans – or some of them – brought upon themselves. Genevans were steadily, surreptitiously, helping to build up the emergent Reformed Church in France. This was deeply subversive from the point of view of France's Catholic monarchy, and the Genevan government generally preferred not to know about this covert aid. On the eve of its own civil Wars of Religion, France and its government was strongly tempted to eradicate the perceived source of division in the kingdom by striking at Geneva.

Fear in the face of such threats to Geneva's survival was countered by a sense of divine protection that clearly derived from Calvin's insistence on God's providence, combined with the right measure of self-help: as the Genevan government told the Savoyards in 1559, they were resolved 'to put [their] trust in God and to keep a sharp watch'.

11

The Genevan Academy

Despite dark clouds at the end of the 1550s, and doubtless inspired by Calvin's conviction of divine protection, Geneva was showing every sign of expansive confidence. In particular, the city launched an ambitious educational venture which formalized its role as the nursery of Reformed Christianity and made it for some years the intellectual dynamo of the Calvinist world. This project was the Academy, founded in 1559 and representing the city's most important enterprise in the fields of secondary and tertiary education. Its establishment and undoubted success meant that, more than ever, Geneva would function as a major international transit centre, receiving visitors, refugees and trainees, sending out missionaries, graduates and starry-eyed admirers. The Academy was John Calvin's pet project. Indeed, he had been pressing for it for some years. In 1550, in the middle of the Perrinist period of Geneva's political history, he was encountering a kind of passive resistance or indifference from the councillors over his academic plans. However, after 1558, following the establishment of Calvin's much more assured position in the city, the council took up his educational project with considerable enthusiasm. Indeed, their minutes suggest that they were trying to present the academic scheme as their own initiative, with 'M. Calvin and other intellectuals' in a merely advisory role. In truth, though, the establishment of the Academy in 1559 was for Calvin – awarded Genevan citizenship that same year –

a personal triumph; his hand can be traced in every stage of the planning of the Academy, especially in the key areas of the selection of faculty and the drawing up of the syllabus.

To staff the Academy, Calvin instinctively looked for the top names in French academia. He did not always get the academic super-stars he wanted: the Professor of Hebrew at Paris's prestigious Collège de France seems to have been strangely reluctant to leave the French capital for a post in a new, untried foundation in faraway Geneva. However, in 1559 Calvin had a piece of good luck in his selection of faculty because of mass resignations of teaching staff at the Academy of Lausanne in Switzerland. These Lausanne lecturers, plus some students, transferred to Calvin's Academy, giving it a strong staffing base.

The teaching staff and the curriculum reflected Calvin's own preferences and his own education in French Christian humanism. Though Geneva paid, with some difficulty, for the Academy, Frenchmen preponderated on the staff, four-fifths of its earliest students were French, and it seems significant that Calvin chose to deliver the Academy's opening address in French rather than the Latin customary on such occasions: though it was un-doubtedly international in its composition, the Genevan Academy operated above all as the unofficial Protestant University of France.

Typical of the Academy's French orientation and the epitome of its educational aims was its rector, the French nobleman Théodore de Bèze (Beza). Calvin's eventual successor in the leadership of the Genevan pastorate. A Greek and Latin poet and translator, Beza was a classicist through and through. But translator as he was of the New Testament into Latin and eventually an editor of the Greek New Testament, he was above all a glittering product of that French tradition of Christian classicism which had formed Calvin and which went back to Jacques Lefèvre d'Étaples.

The Academy's curriculum mirrored its debt to this Christian humanism, with its emphasis on the ancient languages. The insti-tution was divided into two sections, the *schola privata*, really an advanced grammar school for Geneva, and the *schola publica*, the university-related upper section. Whereas the *schola publica* gave a good grounding, as any contemporary decent grammar school in Europe would have done, in classical languages and literature – what Beza called 'liberal studies', the *schola privata* provided advanced courses, in Hebrew and in theology, the traditional queen of subjects, with Calvin taking a chair of theology. The scholar had come home.

12
Calvin: scholar, writer, organizer

Indeed, Calvin's scholarly and teaching work had never really been interrupted. For one thing, he had worked incessantly on his series of scriptural commentaries, which were in fact published lectures. Calvin's main literary and scholarly work – and this includes the *Institutes* – consists largely of scriptural commentaries. Now we might think that the most fruitful periods for that kind of reflective work would have been those spells of seclusion from public affairs, in particular the months before 1541 in enforced absence from his work at Geneva. Indeed, in that period Calvin composed such works as his great tribute to the main source of Reformation theology, *Commentaries on the Epistle of Paul to the Romans*. However, not only did Calvin subsequently find time, amidst the cares of his Genevan ministry, to teach, research, write, and publish, but that kind of work was essential to him above all in the most stressful phases of his career. Then his long hours of study raised his horizons, recalled to him the scholar that he really was, allowed him to speak to an European audience, and fortified him for the almost incessant conflicts that he faced in Geneva between the mid-1540s and the mid-1550s. Indeed, as Professor Parker points out, the years of opposition to Calvin's 'godly society' saw the production of 'new editions of the *Institutes* and commentaries on nearly all the books of the New Testament'. By 1555, Calvin had completed and published his majesty series of commentaries on the Epistles and Gospels of the

New Testament, and had begun the commentaries on the books of the Old Testament on which he worked steadily for the remainder of his life, with a sustained burst of composition between 1557 and 1564.

Calvin's method of working on these books might seem rather roundabout to us, even though it tells us much about him – his urgency, his intimate knowledge of his material and his verbal fluency. His commentaries were in fact mostly lectures to students. Since Calvin seldom had time to write out these lectures beforehand, he delivered them extempore and then relied on his better students to provide him with transcripts of what were in fact superbly structured and entirely articulate productions. These lectures – especially those on the Hebrew Old Testament – also show Calvin's profound linguistic learning and proficiency. Incidentally, the reverential way in which Calvin's words were conserved indicates his growing status as a kind of guru: in just the same way, though with rather less justification, Martin Luther's dinner-table monologues were copied down by his students with rapt concentration.

Only in Calvin's manner of writing is there any whiff of creative eccentricity about him. He did a lot of his work in bed, starting at perhaps five in the morning, and after preaching he would lie 'down on the bed fully clothed and pursue his labours on some book'. However, this was not artistic bohemianism but his way of coping with chronic ill-health, imprecisely diagnosed but generally located in the stomach and lungs. Sickness did not let him off literary labours: quite the reverse, for a dangerous illness in 1558 sent him back to a revision of the *Institutes*, the encyclopedia of his theology. The preparation of this work, or at least the translation of the Latin text into French, was, as Calvin's contemporary biographer, Colladon, recalled, fairly chaotic, and indeed the orderly but always hurried Calvin frequently worked in an apparently helter-skelter way. However, the eventual arrangement of this definitive edition of the *Institutes*, published in 1559, is a model of symmetrical order, its four books being based on the conventional divisions of the Apostles' Creed.

Calvin had dedicated the first edition of the *Institutes* to Francis I of France. This habit of dedication to eminent persons – which was indeed a common sixteenth-century authorial courtesy – stayed with him. His commentary on *I Timothy* was dedicated to England's Protestant regent under the boy king Edward VI (1547–53), Protector Somerset. King Edward himself received a dedication to two of Calvin's commentaries, and Edward's Protestant half-sister, Elizabeth, was sent a fulsome dedication of his commentary on *Isaiah*. His commentary on *Hebrews* went with a dedication to the king of Poland. This selection of dedications exhibits something of the range of Calvin's interests in Europe – he even showed interest in Brazil – and, along with his letters to statesmen such as Somerset, his dedications help identify those areas of Europe where Calvin's movement had hopes of considerable expansion after mid-century. As Calvin consolidated his authority in Geneva – a new version of the *Ecclesiastical Ordinances* in 1561 increased the powers of the Church – so he found more scope for a European role, himself contributing to the vast expansion of his movement after 1559.

Indeed, that year of 1559 was a year of great hope and growth both for Calvin and for his international following. The year of Calvin's receipt of Genevan citizenship, of the setting up of the Academy, and of the definitive edition of the *Institutes* also saw the first national synod of the Reformed Church in France, the abolition of popery and the reintroduction of Reformation into England, and the consolidation of a distinctly Calvinist Reformation in Scotland.

This expansion of his creed across western Europe – and into the centre and east of the Continent too – gives Calvin a stature far above that of those earlier leading figures of the Swiss and German Reformations who worked within the confines of single cities. The Reformation of Geneva was for Calvin of course an important task in its own right, but it was also seen as a model and a first step in preparing for the evangelization of France and of the whole of Christendom. In this respect, and especially considering the centrality of France in the impending religious power struggle in Europe, the year 1559 was, once again, decisive: the accidental death in that year of the oppressively Catholic Henry II of France gravely weakened France's Catholic Valois monarchy, and in that year too Geneva sent out a massive and unprecedented wave of 32 missionaries, all of them to France.

Obviously, the sending of such an organized mission to Europe's senior Catholic kingdom – an action rightly interpreted by the French authorities as highly provocative – indicated that Calvin saw no possibility of any reconciliation with Rome. The fundamentally hostile position he had earlier adopted in the *Letter to Sadoleto* he re-stated in a string of anti-Catholic tracts in the 1540s. The reaffirmation by the Catholic Church's reforming Council of Trent (1545–63) of the essentials of traditional Catholic faith convinced Calvin that Rome was no true Church, and in 1547 he roundly denounced the Council itself. This had been preceded, in 1543, by his vitriolic *Treatise on Relics*, a satiric classic in the Erasmian vein – though it has to be said that the elements of medieval Catholic piety that Calvin pilloried here were also currently under attack from reform-minded Catholic intellectuals. Indeed, to an extent, in works such as the *Treatise*, Calvin was continuing to vilify, with diminishing relevance, features of the late medieval cultic system of his boyhood which were being extensively transformed, if not extinguished, during his adult life.

Because of his powerful conviction of the total falsity of Catholicism, Calvin had no sympathy for bridge-builders or reconcilers, middle positions, fudging or concealment. It is true that bridge-building operations were widely popular in the middle decades of the sixteenth century, partly because Christians were by no means yet adjusted to the spectacle of rival Christianities. Separated by twenty years, the conferences, or colloquies at Regensburg in Germany in 1541 and at Poissy in France in 1561 represented ecumenical attempts to restore Christian unity. They failed, and Calvin was particularly scathing about apparent attempts by leading German Protestant theologians at Regensburg to build bridges by selling passes – to compromise on essentials for the sake of an appearance of unity. He himself concentrated on the alternative task of building unity between Protestant Churches, and here he showed that he could compromise on inessential points where basic assumptions were held in common. His major achievement in this field was the doctrinal union of Swiss Protestant Churches with Geneva in the *Consensus Tigurinus*, or Zürich Agreement, of 1549.

Undoubtedly, there was a major political as well as religious motive underlying would-be unity talks such as those at Regensburg and Poissy: religious discord destroyed the vital unity of political societies, and in Germany, France and elsewhere caused damaging civil wars. Thus in the second half of the sixteenth century there was a vogue for political (in current French, *politique*) solutions to religious problems, playing down theological rifts and emphasizing the need for agreement within states. Calvin, needless to say, was the least *politique* of men, and he addressed a string of letters to the lay leaders of French Protestantism adjuring them to face up to their religious responsibilities and avoid all political compromise in matters of faith. In similar confrontational mode, Calvin urged his followers, especially the high-placed among them, never to sacrifice or conceal their convictions for the sake of personal safety or advancement. In this vein, one of his most characteristic works was his 1544 tract, *Apology of John Calvin to those Gentlemen the Nicodemites* (the word being an allusion to Jesus's timid and clandestine disciple, Nicodemus). Calvin castigated as blasphemy the Nicodemites' 'human prudence' which led them 'to convince themselves that the way really to further the gospel is to take part in the papists' idolatry'.

Calvin, then, was himself a deeply embattled leader and, for all his scholar's loathing for war, he breathed the authentic spirit of militancy that hovered like a heavy thunder cloud over France in the build-up to the tragic Wars of Religion which finally broke out in 1562. It is indeed true that Calvin, in terms to be expected from a Christian pastor, uttered explicit warnings against the use of force. However, the whole tenor of his teaching was in the direction of resistance and confrontation, and indeed of active political conflict with Catholic authorities, especially in France. In the first place, his classical learning supplied him with historical examples, in Athens, for example, of citizens' rights to resist tyranny; then his knowledge of French institutions induced him to see parallels between those ancient guardians of liberty and the estates of the realm of France; further, his awareness of developments in his homeland led him to look for deliverance from tyranny to the increasing numbers of French nobles who were flocking to the Calvinist banner; and his religious viewpoint brought him to equate a tyranny which might and ought to be resisted with the religious oppressions of France's Catholic monarchy. Calvin unquestionably supplied ideological motor power to the Calvinist offensive in France – whether we see that offensive as protective or aggressive – and he went on to organize aid for France's Huguenot (i.e. Calvinist) insurgents and to deplore what he saw as a sell-out truce they made, near the end of his life, in 1563.

13
Finale

Perhaps had Calvin lived to see the agony of his beloved France through decades of religious warfare, he would have moderated the uncompromisingly adversarial tone that he had used in pieces such as the *Apology to the Nicodemites*. With the Wars of Religion well under way, Calvin, in his mid-50s, looked and was old, bowed down by a lifetime's overwork and a settled anxiety state, in constant, unappeased pain. His acute terminal illness brought out more sharply than ever the human miracle of John Calvin: the work that went on almost to the end, as it had done throughout a strenuous life, regardless of physical strength or weakness; the adamantine mind and steely will that seemed to function almost independent of a useless body. And since Calvin's mind did not seem to require his body's services, it is not at all surprising that that mind remained, as the Geneva council minutes put it, 'whole and entire in sense and understanding'. Indeed, this power of the forceful mind over the wasted matter of his body impressed even Calvin himself: 'it seems as if God wants to concentrate all my inward senses'. After what sounds like a sad and awkward final meeting with city councillors, Calvin met his fellow pastors. In a lengthy but apparently impromptu speech, he reviewed his career at Geneva, considering it chiefly in terms of the conflicts he had faced. There was the occasional characteristically sardonic aside, and throughout the speech a builder's warning against tampering with the structure he had erected, even with all its imperfections. This was not conservatism: Calvin was no more conservative than Robespierre or Lenin. It was simply the revolutionary's anxiety that his revolution remain intact. Calvin died on the evening of 27 May 1564 and was buried, with characteristic physical self-effacement, in a virtually unmarked grave. A genius of ice and fire, through his life's work he permitted the Reformation to survive and expand; no other sixteenth-century figure – not even his mentor, Luther – left as long a legacy as he.

14

The expansion of Calvinism

The first point to make here is that this caption contains a fallacy according to the assumptions of the sixteenth and seventeenth centuries. A term like Calvinism assumes an ideology linked inseparably and uniquely with a single individual, who, though no doubt influenced by others, has created an original and distinctive thought-system. That was not how Calvin and his followers viewed their beliefs, which they saw as the restored consensus of pure Christianity. What we call Calvinism was to Calvinists simply the true Reformation of Christianity, and the term the Calvinists preferred for themselves was the 'Reformed'.

Both before and after John Calvin's death, his ideas spread rapidly and extensively in Europe and beyond. Indeed, the Calvinist Reformation had an expansive capacity largely denied to the earlier Lutheran movement whose spread was mostly confined to German territories and Scandinavia. Although he was deeply concerned with the evangelization of France, Calvin wrote for a fully international audience, using the international languages of French and Latin. He operated from a strategically placed Free City which lay on important crossroads and which both attracted visitors from throughout Europe and sent out emissaries to all corners. In addition, the Calvinist Church system, evolved for Geneva, was an immensely exportable one. The Lutherans' entrenched political deference and reluctance to disobey constituted authorities meant that the Lutheran

Reformation was established largely where ruling princes and city authorities wanted it to be. In contrast, Calvin had fought long and hard in Geneva to secure considerable independence for the Church from the state. Thus were created highly resilient forms of ecclesiastical organization which could be set up, beyond Geneva, whether or not the political authorities approved. In addition, the Genevan system, designed for one city and its dependent territory, could be adapted to the larger needs of great states. These two points – resilience in the face of political prohibition and the organizational adaptability of the Genevan Church order – can be seen clearly in the case of France. There, despite years of heavy state persecution, a fully-fledged federal Calvinist Church organization was set up in 1559 through an elaboration of the Genevan system so as to meet the needs of a vast kingdom.

To what sort of people, in social terms, did Calvinism appeal? A partial answer is that Calvin's ideas had an appeal that cut across class lines and embraced, for instance, senior French and English noblemen and women, country gentry families from England to Poland and Hungary, students and clerics, artisans, merchants and professionals, and even peasants. Indeed, a peasant Calvinism emerged, for instance in some regions of France such as the Cévennes. Here, however, we must enter a reservation. Figures we have for the social composition of a Calvinist congregation in Montpellier in France in the 1560s show strong support from the middling and upper reaches of society but rapidly diminishing allegiance as we reach the ranks of the peasantry: peasant commitment to the congregation was in a kind of inverse ratio to the vast numerical strength of the peasantry in French society. Of course, Montpellier was a city, in which peasants would not in any case preponderate. But it is that urban location of the Montpellier congregation that makes it so typical of the Calvinist movement, not least in France. A product of urban Geneva and destined for a great future in some of northern Europe's greatest cities, Calvinism tended to lack rural appeal. One of its strengths – that it spread through the printed word – was a potential weakness in the heavily pre-literate countryside of early modern France, and of Europe in general. Then, too, it is possible that Calvinism had a diminished rural appeal because it played down that miraculous world-view, of supernatural control over nature, of saints and relics, which to Europe's peasants was, at least psychologically, essential.

The period from about 1560 to the end of the sixteenth century is one of great drama in European history as the religious fate of much of the Continent was finally decided. The religious coloration of much of northern Europe was in fact already fixed: Scandinavia and great tracts of Germany were Lutheran, England and Scotland adopted the Reformation in 1559–60. The religious affiliation of the Mediterranean South was, likewise, settled: Spain, Portugal and Italy had been, or were rapidly becoming, consolidated for Catholicism. However, in a vital middle band of territories and states running across the Continent the eventual religious outcome still had to be decided, including some of Europe's most populous, wealthy and politically important areas. Within this territorial zone, in France and the Netherlands, life-and-death struggles were to take place to establish the forms of Christianity to be practised by whole societies.

In these vital struggles, Calvinism possessed powerful assets, especially in comparison with earlier forms of the Reformation such as Lutheranism and Zwinglianism. As it became established in German and Scandinavian states, Lutheranism increasingly relied on close collaboration with state authorities in such matters as the maintenance of standards of doctrinal education. This alliance with the state had obvious advantages for Lutheran Churches, but it carried with it the disadvantage that Lutheranism could hardly take root where the political authorities were unsympathetic. Calvinism, in contrast, was prone to be more questioning about state power and Calvin himself was often critical of monarchy. Prepared to resist state suppression, Calvinism also had its own organization which was completely independent of the state. At the base of this organization was the local congregation, with its pastor and elders. Lay and clerical deputies from congregations assembled periodically in area bodies called by terms such as 'classes' or 'synods'; these then led up to provincial conferences and at the apex of the pyramid a national assembly. This kind of structure was evolved in France, in the teeth of official repression, during the 1550s. Perhaps fifty local congregations were embraced in the system. In 1559, the capstone of the pyramid, the national assembly, was put in place.

An important feature of the Calvinist structure was its lay element. Through the offices of lay elder and deacon, laymen gained experience in Church government and made up for shortages in the numbers of professional clerics. As we shall see, a particularly important lay element in European Calvinism in the second half of the sixteenth century was made up of aristocratic adherents. Perhaps some of Calvinism's lay cadres – and clerics too – were all too ready to identify themselves as God's elect. Such confidence, however, was the indispensable prerequisite for morale-building in sixteenth-century Europe's most militant – indeed, its most revolutionary – force.

One of the preconditions for the expansion of Calvinism was aristocratic support and protection. Over most of Europe, the sixteenth century saw the expansion of royal power in states. This growth of royal authority was achieved partly at the expense of traditional nobilities, and it is possible to identify a set of rearguard resistance movements by national aristocracies against the rise of centralised monarchical states. Professor Elliott speaks of 'aristocratic constitutionalism', a political outlook which sought a counterbalance to the powers of the royal state in the constitutional rights of nobility. Calvinist political thought linked up with this 'aristocratic constitutionalism', giving it an important religious dimension. Calvin himself made a major contribution to this coalescence. In the 1536 *Institutes*, he had put aristocratic government (and democracy) on an equal footing with monarchy. Despite his habit of dedicating books to monarchs, he had what has been called 'a profound mistrust of monarchy', which he thought prone to tyranny. As a check to such tyrannical possibilities (which he believed he saw being realized in the repression of Protestants by the French crown), Calvin recommended the ancient Greek and Roman models of 'magistrates . . . appointed to curb the tyranny of kings'. Calvin was conservative enough not to call for an indiscriminate right of popular resistance to the state, but his preference for constituted, recognized estates as a block to royal tyranny gave the seal of his approval to 'aristocratic constitutionalism'.

Some of the effects of this can be seen in Europe in the second half of the sixteenth century. In France, the onward march of the royal (and Catholic) state was opposed, in the Wars of Religion (1562–1598), by a Calvinist resistance movement led by such nobles as Louis Prince de Condé (d. 1569) and Gaspard de Coligny. In the neighbouring Netherlands, too, the national uprising against Spain beginning in the mid-1560s was spearheaded by Calvinist nobles: the aristocratic leader of the patriotic movement, William of Orange (1533–1584), converted to Calvinism in recognition of the importance of the Reformed faith for the national struggle. In Scotland, a Calvinist Reformation was established, in opposition to a Catholic

63

monarchy, by an alliance between the reformer John Knox (1505–1572) and the aristocratic Calvinist 'Lords of the Congregation'. In both Poland and Hungary, noble patronage, protection and support were vital to the establishment of what has been termed 'estate Calvinism'.

The connection between Calvinism and aristocracy that is so prominent a feature in Europe in the second half of the sixteenth century did not necessarily last. In Poland, for example, the Catholic Jesuit order took over control of aristocratic education and in the seventeenth century the country's nobility became overwhelmingly Catholic. In France, the nobility's challenge to the crown in the Wars of Religion was eventually repulsed. The seventeenth century saw an impressive revival of royal power and an emphatic renewal of the monarchy's commitment to Catholicism. Calvinism became a real barrier to social prestige and political power, and France's nobility quickly abandoned earlier affiliations to the Reformed faith.

The result, in France and elsewhere, was gradually to give seventeenth-century Calvinism a middle class aura. More specifically, Calvinist religion was coming to be linked to urban middle-class commerce. Observers noted, for example, that virtually all trade in French provincial centres like Toulouse and Rochefort was in the hands of Calvinists. Something similar was apparent in England. There, an influential Calvinist movement had attracted considerable aristocratic and gentry support. Indeed, in the civil wars of the 1640s England had its own version of the earlier French Wars of Religion: a politically aggressive anti-Calvinist monarchy faced an armed resistance movement whose backbone was made up of Calvinist nobles and gentry. In 1660, England's Anglican monarchy was triumphantly restored. Calvinism was in effect proscribed; the universities and much of public life were closed to professing Calvinists who now became second-class citizens. In the years after 1660 most of the families of the landed ruling class that had earlier sponsored the Calvinist movement distanced themselves from what had now become an unfashionable and inconvenient creed. English Calvinism did not die, but it became, as Calvinism had in France, increasingly identified with an urban and commercial bourgeoisie. During anti-Calvinist riots in London in 1710 hostile slogans linked the Calvinist Presbyterians with the unpopular Bank of England. In the popular mind at least, a connection had been made between finance, trade and Calvinist religion.

The great economic success story of the seventeenth century was the Dutch Republic, with its control of Europe's carrying trade, its influential innovations in banking and its lucrative overseas trading empire. This was also a state founded under Calvinist auspices and a society in which Calvinist influences were pervasive. Surely, it was no mere coincidence that this enterprise culture was also one that bore the stamp of Calvin; surely there was a link of some kind between commercial enterprise and Calvinism.

Such a link was eventually identified analytically, and an explanation for it offered, by the pioneer German sociologist Max Weber in his *The Protestant Ethic and the Spirit of Capitalism* (1904–5). Weber hypothesised that key features of Calvinist theology, above all the belief in predestination, were stimuli towards economic success. The typical Calvinist, Weber thought, was anxious to know whether or not he was of the saved elect. He constantly sought proofs of God's approval in his worldly success, but in fact himself achieved that worldly success – often in the commercial field – through unremitting effort.

As may be imagined, Weber's hypotheses, which were put forward with great caution, have been subjected to critical discussion. It is not possible here to reach any firm conclusions about Weber's thesis. However, the following points can be made. John Calvin himself was on the whole suspicious of commercial and financial activity, preferring something akin to what medieval moralists called 'holy poverty'. Notwithstanding this, later generations of Calvinists have undoubtedly played a leading role, as entrepreneurs, in the economic and industrial development of such societies as the Netherlands, Britain, and the United States. In some social contexts – England after 1660, for instance – Calvinists were channelled towards business and away from other educational, professional and political avenues of opportunity. At the same time, Calvinists were encouraged by their puritanical moral code to be frugal, thrifty, and industrious in the 'callings' to which God had ordained them. In England and Scotland they developed admirable educational systems which laid down the foundations for career success. Many of the reasons for the Calvinist economic miracle can be found in the factors considered here, so that we do not need to look too far into the inner recesses of Calvinist theology in our search for an explanation of the link between Calvinist convictions and economic enterprise and success.

We have seen that Calvinism during the sixteenth century and later made a major contribution to movements of protest and liberation. We have also seen something of the contribution of Calvinism and Calvinists to the economic development of western Europe since the sixteenth century. Clearly, the religious movement that John Calvin launched from Geneva has been one of the most potent forces in European history in the last four hundred years.

Suggested further reading

There are a number of good, reliable survey works on the age of the Reformation: H. G. Koenigsberger and George L. Mosse, *Europe in the Sixteenth Century* (1968, London: Longmans, especially chapter VII); G. R. Elton, *Reformation Europe 1517–1559* (1968, London: Collins, Fontana History of Europe, especially chapter VIII); *The New Cambridge Modern History*, Volume II. *The Reformation 1520–1550*, edited by G. R. Elton (1962, Cambridge: Cambridge University Press, especially chapter IV, section I.) Two concise readable textbooks on the Reformation context are: A. G. Dickens, *Reformation and Society in Sixteenth-Century Europe* (1966, London: Thames and Hudson, especially chapter VIII), and Joel Hurstfield (ed.) *The Reformation Crisis* (1965, London. Edward Arnold, especially chapter III).

On Christian humanism, see S. Dresden, *Humanism in the Renaissance* (trans. Margaret King, 1968, London: Weidenfeld and Nicolson, World University Library, especially chapters 2 and 3).

A good, sympathetic, not over-long biography is by T. H. L. Parker, *John Calvin: A Biography* (1977, Philadelphia, Westminster University Press). William J. Bouwsma's *John Calvin. A Sixteenth Century Portrait* (1988, New York and Oxford: Oxford University Press) is the finest modern study. For Calvin's theology, see the collection of eleven essays by F. L. Battles and others, *John Calvin* (1966, Courtenay Studies in Reformation Theology I, Abingdon, Berks., Sutton Courtenay Press). A standard work on Calvin's doctrines is François Wendel, *Calvin. The Origins and Development of his Religious Thought* (trans. Philip Mairet, 1963, London: Collins, The Fontana Library of Theology and Philosophy). For Calvin's politics, see Harro Höpfl, *The Christian Polity of John Calvin* (1982, Cambridge: Cambridge University Press).

Calvinism's expansion, in Europe and America, is surveyed in Menna Prestwick (ed.) *International Calvinism 1541–1715* (1985, Oxford: Clarendon Press, see in particular the last chapter on the Weber thesis). Note also the earlier work by John T. McNeill, *The History and Character of Calvinism* (1954, New York: Oxford University Press).

There are some helpful collections of documents, including Hans J. Hillerbrand, *The Reformation in its Own Words* (1964, London: S.C.M. Press, especially section IV). John Dillenberger offers extensive excerpts from Calvin, especially from the *Institutes*, in *John Calvin. Selections from his Writings* (1971, New York: Anchor Books).